THE THIRTEEN COLONIES

South Carolina

CRAIG A. DOHERTY

KATHERINE M. DOHERTY

Facts On File, Inc.

South Carolina

Facts On File, Inc.
132 West 31st Street
New York NY 10001

Library of Congress Cataloging-in-Publication Data
Doherty, Craig A.
    South Carolina / Craig A. Doherty and Katherine M. Doherty.
                              p. cm.—(Thirteen colonies)
    Includes bibliographical references and index.
    ISBN 0-8160-5409-6 (acid-free paper)
    1. South Carolina—History—Colonial period, ca. 1600–1775—Juvenile literature.
    2. South Carolina—History—1775–1865—Juvenile literature. I. Doherty, Katherine
M. II. Title.

    F272.D64 2005
    975.7'02—dc22   2004001069

Facts On File books are available at special discounts when purchased in bulk quantities for businesses, associations, institutions, or sales promotions. Please call our Special Sales Department in New York at (212) 967-8800 or (800) 322-8755.

You can find Facts On File on the World Wide Web at http://www.factsonfile.com

Text design by Erika K. Arroyo
Cover design by Semadar Megged
Maps and graph by Sholto Ainslie

Printed in the United States of America

VB Hermitage 10 9 8 7 6 5 4 3 2 1

This book is printed on acid-free paper.

Contents

Note on Photos

Many of the illustrations and photographs used in this book are old, historical images. The quality of the prints is not always up to current standards, as in some cases the originals are from old or poor quality negatives or are damaged. The content of the illustrations, however, made their inclusion important despite problems in reproduction.

Introduction

In the 11th century, Vikings from Scandinavia sailed to North America. They explored the Atlantic coast and set up a few small settlements. In Newfoundland and Nova Scotia, Canada, archaeologists have found traces of these settlements. No one knows for sure why they did not establish permanent colonies. It may have been that it was too far away from their homeland. At about the same time, many Scandinavians were involved with raiding and establishing settlements along the coasts of what are now Great Britain and France. This may have offered greater rewards than traveling all the way to North America.

When the western part of the Roman Empire fell in 476, Europe lapsed into a period of almost 1,000 years of wars, plagues, and hardship. This period of European history is often referred to as the Dark Age or Middle Ages. Communication between the different parts of Europe was almost nonexistent. If other Europeans knew about the Vikings' explorations westward, they left no record of it. Between the time of Viking exploration and Christopher Columbus's 1492 journey, Europe underwent many changes.

By the 15th century, Europe had experienced many advances. Trade within the area and with the Far East had created prosperity for the governments and many wealthy people. The Catholic Church had become a rich and powerful institution. Although wars would be fought and governments would come and go, the countries of Western Europe had become fairly strong. During this time, Europe rediscovered many of the arts and sciences that had

Vikings explored the Atlantic coast of North America in ships similar to this one. *(National Archives of Canada)*

existed before the fall of Rome. They also learned much from their trade with the Near and Far East. Historians refer to this time as the Renaissance, which means "rebirth."

At this time, some members of the Catholic Church did not like the direction the church was going. People such as Martin Luther and John Calvin spoke out against the church. They soon gained a number of followers who decided that they would protest and form their own churches. The members of these new churches were called Protestants. The movement to establish these new churches is called the Protestant Reformation. It would have a big impact on America as many Protestant groups would leave Europe so they could worship the way they wanted to.

In addition to religious dissent, problems arose with the overland trade routes to the Far East. The Ottoman Turks took control of the lands in the Middle East and disrupted trade. It was at this time that European explorers began trying to find a water route to the Far East. The explorers first sailed around Africa. Then an Italian named Christopher Columbus convinced the king and queen of Spain that it would be shorter to sail west to Asia rather than go around Africa. Most sailors and educated people at the time knew the world was round. However, Columbus made two errors in his calculations. First, he did not realize just how big the Earth is, and second, he did not know that the continents of North and South America blocked a westward route to Asia.

When Columbus made landfall in 1492, he believed that he was in the Indies, as the Far East was called at the time. For a period of time after Columbus, the Spanish controlled the seas and the exploration of what was called the New World. England tried to compete with the Spanish on the high seas, but their ships were no match for the floating fortresses of the Spanish Armada. These heavy ships, known as galleons, ruled the Atlantic.

In 1588, that all changed. A fleet of English ships fought a series of battles in which their smaller but faster and more maneuverable ships finally defeated the Spanish Armada. This opened up the New World to anyone willing to cross the ocean. Portugal, Holland, France, and England all funded voyages of exploration to the New World. In North America, the French explored the far north. The Spanish had already established colonies in what are now Florida, most of the Caribbean, and much of Central and South America. The Dutch bought Manhattan and would establish what would

Depicted in this painting, Christopher Columbus completed three additional voyages to the Americas after his initial trip in search of a westward route to Asia in 1492. *(Library of Congress, Prints and Photographs Division [LC-USZ62-103980])*

Composed of large, heavy ships known as galleons, the Spanish Armada, seen here in an early 17th-century engraving, was a formidable enemy of the English during the 16th century. The Spanish ruled the seas with this floating fortress until their defeat by the more maneuverable English fleet. *(Library of Congress, Prints and Photographs Division [LC-USZ62-86540])*

become New York, as well as various islands in the Caribbean and lands in South America. The English claimed most of the east coast of North America and set about creating colonies in a variety of ways.

Companies were formed in England and given royal charters to set up colonies. Some of the companies sent out military and trade expeditions to find gold and other riches. They employed men such as John Smith, Bartholomew Gosnold, and others to explore the lands they had been granted. Other companies found groups of Protestants who wanted to leave England and worked out deals that let them establish colonies. No matter what circumstances a colony was established under, the first settlers suffered hardships as they tried to build communities in what to them was a wilderness. They also had to deal with the people who were already there.

Native Americans lived in every corner of the Americas. There were vast and complex civilizations in Central and South America. The city that is now known as Cahokia was located along the Mississippi River in what is today Illinois and may have had as many as 50,000 residents. The people of Cahokia built huge earthen mounds that can still be seen today. There has been a lot of speculation as to the total population of Native Americans in 1492. Some have put the number as high as 40 million people.

Most of the early explorers encountered Native Americans. They often wrote descriptions of them for the people of Europe. They also kidnapped a few of these people, took them back to Europe, and put them on display. Despite the number of Native Americans, the Europeans still claimed the land as their own. The rulers of Europe and the Catholic Church at the time felt they had a right to take any lands they wanted from people who did not share their level of technology and who were not Christians.

The Thirteen Colonies, 1790

Quebec

Lake Superior

Lake Michigan

Lake Huron

Lake Ontario

Lake Erie

Mississippi R.

Northwest Territory

Miami R.

Muskingum R.

Ohio R.

Kanawha R.

St. Lawrence R.

claimed by United States and Britain

Maine (Massachusetts)

New Hampshire
June 21, 1788

Massachusetts
February 6, 1788

New York
July 26, 1788

Rhode Island
May 29, 1790

Connecticut
January 9, 1788

Pennsylvania
December 12, 1787

New Jersey
December 18, 1787

Delaware
December 7, 1787

Maryland
April 28, 1788

Virginia
June 25, 1788

Louisiana

Mississippi R.

Territory South
of the Ohio River

North Carolina
November 21, 1789

South Carolina
May 23, 1788

Georgia
January 2, 1788

*ATLANTIC
OCEAN*

claimed by Spain,
United States, and Georgia

West Florida

East
Florida

N

Gulf of Mexico

	United States
	U.S. territory
	British territory
	Spanish territory
	Disputed territory

May 23,
1788 — Date state ratified
the Constitution

0   200 miles

0   200 km

First Contacts

EARLY EXPLORERS

The land that is now South Carolina was an area of conflicting claims among the countries of Europe shortly after Christopher Columbus found his way to the West Indies in 1492. Based on Columbus's voyage, Spain laid claim to most of the Western Hemisphere, and the Spanish were the first to land on the Carolina coast and try to settle there. The English also claimed much of the area. John Cabot sailed west from England in 1497, and he explored the coast of North America from Greenland south. It is believed that he headed back to England after sailing south to about latitude 38°, somewhere off the Virginia coast.

Although Cabot probably did not get as far south as the Carolinas, England claimed the territory anyway. At the time, what a country claimed was not as important as what they could settle and defend. As it turned out, claiming the land of what is today South Carolina was far easier than creating a colony there.

In addition to the Spanish and English, the French also claimed this same area. In 1525, Giovanni da Verrazano, who was an Italian sailing for the French, claimed much of North America for France. Over the next 150 years, there were a number of attempts to colonize the area that the Spanish called Carolana, which in Latin means "land of Charles." Charles I was king of Spain at the time, and the land was named in his honor.

In the early 1500s, the Spanish were successful in establishing a number of colonies on the islands of the Caribbean and in Central and South America. Their colonies depended on the enslavement of

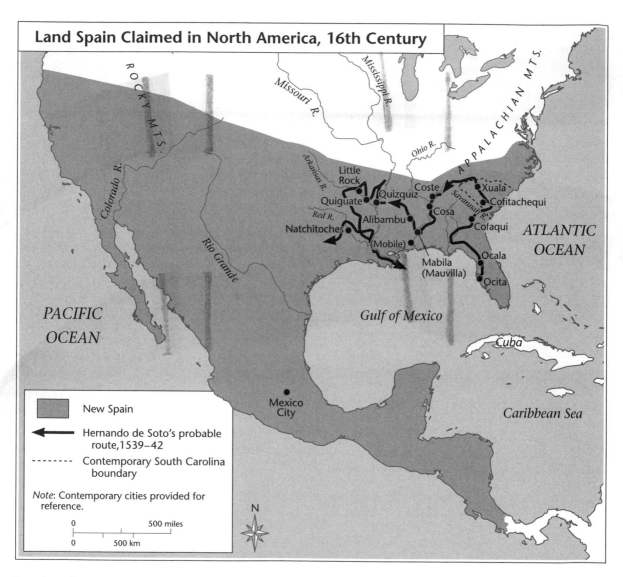

Land Spain Claimed in North America, 16th Century

ROCKY MTS.

Missouri R.

Mississippi R.

APPALACHIAN MTS.

Ohio R.

Arkansas R.

Colorado R.

Rio Grande

Red R.

Little Rock

Quiguate

Quizquiz

Coste

Xuala

Cofitachequi

Natchitoches

Alibambu

Cosa

Savannah R.

Cofaqui

ATLANTIC OCEAN

(Mobile)

Mabila (Mauvilla)

Ocala

Ocita

PACIFIC OCEAN

Gulf of Mexico

Cuba

Mexico City

Caribbean Sea

Legend

New Spain

Hernando de Soto's probable route, 1539–42

Contemporary South Carolina boundary

Note: Contemporary cities provided for reference.

0   500 miles

0   500 km

N

Based on the travels of a number of Spanish explorers, Spain claimed a large portion of North America, which included what is now South Carolina.

the Native American people they found there. No one has been able to give an accurate number to the population of Native Americans in 1492. However, the best estimates today suggest that there were far more Native Americans than was previously thought. It is now believed that Hispaniola, which is the second largest island in the Caribbean, may have had as many as 8 million Native Americans in

Francisco Chicora

Francisco Chicora learned to speak Spanish while a prisoner and was soon telling amazing stories about the land he came from. The Spanish recorded some of these stories in their journals. One of the most often repeated stories attributed to Chicora was that there was a race of people in Carolana who had long thick tails. To sit down, they had to make a hole in the ground for their tails.

Another story was about a group of giants who got that way by stretching their children. The story the Spanish found most interesting was of the great treasure that existed in Carolana. One will never know why Chicora told these stories. It may be that he hoped it would somehow get him back to his home, which is what happened. He was taken on the expedition to Carolana to act as a guide and interpreter. As soon as he could, he ran away from the Spanish, who never found the giants, people with tails, or the treasure Chicora had told them about.

1492. However, slavery and European disease reduced that number to a few hundred in less than 100 years.

As the Native American population in the islands was drastically reduced, the Spanish began to import slaves from Africa and Native Americans from other areas. The first documented contact between the Spanish and the Native Americans in Carolana was a voyage in 1521 led by Francisco Gordillo and sponsored by Lucas Vázquez de Ayllón, a government official in Hispaniola. Gordillo sailed with two ships from Hispaniola to the mouth of the Pee Dee River, where the modern town of Georgetown, South Carolina, is situated.

There Gordillo tricked a number of Native Americans onto his ship by offering them gifts. When he had about 150 people on the ship, he sailed off with them. Many of them died on the way back to Hispaniola. Gordillo taught Spanish to one of these captives and named him Francisco Chicora. It was Chicora who created interest in settling Carolana by telling stories about his homeland.

FIRST SETTLEMENTS

After hearing the fantastic stories of Francisco Chicora, Lucas Vázquez de Ayllón decided to start a colony in Carolana. In 1526, he gathered together 500 people and six ships and then headed north to the area visited by Gordillo. Ayllón brought Francisco Chicora and some of the

Shown in an illustration published in 1892, Hernando de Soto and a force of 600 people explored what is now the southeastern United States, killing American Indians and destroying their villages as they traveled. *(Library of Congress, Prints and Photographs Division [LC-USZ62-104329])*

other Native Americans who had been kidnapped by Gordillo to serve as guides and interpreters. Very little was recorded about this first attempt to start a colony in South Carolina.

It is known that the largest ship in the small fleet ran aground off the Carolana coast and sank with a large portion of the colonists' supplies. The Native Americans took their first opportunity and disappeared into the swamps and forests of the coast. There is no record of the exact location of the attempted colony. It is believed that Ayllón died of fever after only a short time in Carolana.

Those who remained had trouble surviving. Fever and attacks by Native Americans killed many. A mutiny by some of the survivors created even more problems. When the remnants of the group returned to Hispaniola, more than 350 members of the failed colony had died. No Europeans remained behind in Carolana.

The next Europeans to visit the area were part of a Spanish expedition led by Hernando de Soto. De Soto and a force of 600 men landed near what is now Tampa Bay, Florida, in May 1539. From there, they traveled north along the coast of the Gulf of Mexico. The reports from the time have conflicting details, but it is believed that he and his men traveled throughout what is now the southeastern quarter of the United States, including what are now the states of Florida, Alabama, Georgia, South Carolina, North Carolina, Tennessee, Mississippi, Oklahoma, Arkansas, Louisiana, and Texas.

De Soto used his small army to take whatever he needed or wanted from the Native Americans whom he met along the way. When the Native Americans resisted, de Soto had his men kill them and burn their villages. In one village in what is now South Carolina, he met up with a Native American woman who was the leader of her people. She is known as the "Lady of Cofitachequi."

Lady of Cofitachequi

De Soto found a strong confederation of Native American tribes in South Carolina known as the Cofitachequi. It is believed that their confederation extended from the coast to the foothills of the Appalachians. When de Soto did not find any gold or silver, he forced the Cofitachequi to provide him with food and people to carry it. De Soto wrote about the Lady of Cofitachequi, who was one of the leaders of the group. When he left the area, he kidnapped the woman and forced her to accompany his expedition. When de Soto was crossing the mountains, the Lady of Cofitachequi managed to escape. Within 150 years, the strong Cofitachequi Confederation had completely disappeared.

De Soto never made it back from his trip. He died of fever on May 21, 1542, near the junctions of the Canadian and Arkansas Rivers in present-day Oklahoma. Fearing attacks from Native Americans if they learned that de Soto had died, his men kept his death a secret. Instead of burying him, they weighted his body down and slipped it into a river.

At one time, historians wrote about de Soto as a great explorer who helped create interest in settling the southeastern corner of North America. However, today de Soto is seen as a greedy and despotic explorer who did immense harm to the Native Americans, whom he exposed to European diseases. Some of the Native American groups of the lower Mississippi River basin quickly died out from the smallpox epidemic that de Soto left behind.

It was another 40 years before Europeans again tried to establish a colony in South Carolina. In 1562, Jean Ribault was granted permission by the admiral of France, Gaspard de Coligny, to start a colony in the lands claimed for France by Verrazano in 1524. Coligny and the French had two goals in mind for starting a colony in Carolana. First, they needed a place to send French Protestants, called Huguenots, who were causing problems in Catholic France. Also, the Spanish were shipping large quantities of gold, silver, and other valuables from their American colonies back to Spain. The best route to Europe brought the treasure ships along the Carolana coast. A colony there could be used as a base to attack Spanish shipping.

Leader of the Cofitachequi people, who may have lived near the Savannah River, the "Lady of Cofitachequi" was taken prisoner by Hernando de Soto after providing him and his fellow explorers with supplies. Depicted here in a late 19th-century engraving, she escaped, but her people disappeared by the end of the 17th century. *(Library of Congress, Prints and Photographs Division [LC-USZ62-104319])*

Ribault's first attempt at establishing a colony was a disaster. He and his men came to a large bay, which they named Port Royal Sound. It is still called that today. There they built Charlesfort, a small fort where the 26 men Ribault left behind could defend themselves while he returned to France for more settlers.

Huguenots

Like the Puritans in England, the Huguenots in France were Protestants. At first, they were tolerated by the Catholic majority. At one point, as many as one-quarter of the people in France converted to Protestantism. Many of the nobility and upper classes became Huguenots. Between 1562 and 1598, toleration ended, and there were eight wars between French Huguenots and French Catholics. During this time, many Huguenots left France. Some came to the Americas in search of religious freedom.

Sponsored by Admiral of France Gaspard de Coligny, Jean Ribault sailed to Carolana with plans to found a colony to serve as a home for Huguenots, or French Protestants, and as a base from which the French could attack Spanish ships sailing from the American colonies to Spain. This engraving depicts Ribault's second expedition as it enters St. Johns River in Florida. *(Library of Congress, Prints and Photographs Division [LC-USZ62-60966])*

In 1562, Jean Ribault erected the column in this illustration, portrayed as an object of worship for Native Americans, during his first expedition to Carolana. René Goulaine de Laudonnière (far right) accompanied Ribault on his first expedition and later returned with another group to build Fort Caroline. De Laudonnière is shown here with Timucuan chief Athore. *(Library of Congress, Prints and Photographs Division [LC-USZ62-374])*

The men left behind did little work. Rather than plant crops, they traded for food with local Native Americans. When they grew dissatisfied with the man Ribault left in charge, they mutinied. They then built a boat and tried to sail back to France using their clothes and bedding for sails. At sea, the men ran out of food and water. It is thought that they resorted to cannibalism before they were rescued by an English ship.

Despite the failure of his first colony, Ribault was determined to create a place for the Huguenots in America. When he returned to France, he found the country embroiled in civil war between the Huguenots and the Catholics. The English were supporting the Huguenot side, and Ribault asked them for help with his attempt to establish a colony. Instead, they put him in prison.

While Ribault was in prison in England, Coligny sponsored another attempt at a colony in 1565. René Goulaine de Laudonnière, who had sailed to America with Ribault on his first voyage, led a group to the St. Johns River in Florida. There they built Fort Caroline. The small colony was about to suffer the same fate as Charlesfort when Ribault, who had been released from prison in England, arrived with supplies and reinforcements.

At the same time, the Spanish were establishing a fort at St. Augustine in Florida. The leader of the Spanish at St. Augustine, Pedro Menéndez de Avilés, had orders to drive the French out of the lands they claimed. Ribault learned of Menéndez's plans and went to sea to attack St. Augustine. Ribault's ships were scattered by a storm while Menéndez marched up the coast and attacked Fort Caroline. The Spanish killed the French soldiers they captured. Later they found Ribault shipwrecked along the coast and executed him and his remaining men.

Menéndez then set about building a Spanish fort in Carolana in 1566. Fort San Felipe was built on what is today Parris Island. Spain's plan was to hold the coastline of Florida and Carolana so that pirates and privateers would not be able to use it as a base to attack the Spanish treasure ships.

Except for being abandoned for a few years in the 1570s because of attacks by Native Americans, San Felipe remained the northernmost outpost of Spain on the Atlantic Coast. That changed when the Englishman, Sir Francis Drake, attacked and burned St. Augustine. Although Drake

Pedro Menéndez de Avilés helped establish the fort at St. Augustine in Florida. *(Library of Congress, Prints and Photographs Division [LC-USZ62-102263])*

Pirates, Privateers, and Spanish Treasure

In the 16th century, Spain ruled the oceans and was the richest and most powerful country in Europe. Much of Spain's wealth came from its colonies in Central and South America. The gold and silver from Spain's American mines and the goods that came in to support the Spanish colonies were tempting targets.

Privateers, who sailed privately owned ships in the employ of a government, were sent out to attack the shipping of Spain.

They attacked cities in the Caribbean and the treasure ships sailing back to Spain. The best route to Europe took the ships up the Gulf Stream past the Carolina coast. It was here that shipping was often attacked.

When there was peace in Europe, pirates, who were out to steal fortunes for themselves, used the Carolina coast as a base. In the early days of Charleston, pirates often traded with the settlers there.

did not directly attack San Felipe, the people there were left in a vulnerable position, and the colony was abandoned. Spanish Carolana was left to its many Native American inhabitants for the next 50 years or more.

2

The Native Americans of South Carolina

It is difficult to give an accurate picture of the Native Americans of South Carolina just before their contact with Europeans. Early explorers such as de Soto and Gordillo did not have enough contact with the original people of South Carolina to leave much of a record of them. Shortly after these earliest contacts, disease spread rapidly throughout the Native American groups of the Southeast and killed untold numbers of people. As soon as trade began between the Native Americans and Europeans, there was a rapid technology change as the Native Americans adopted European tools, weapons, and cloth. However, there is much that is known about the culture, languages, and tribal groups in South Carolina in the 16th century.

THE TRIBES OF SOUTH CAROLINA

The best estimates suggest that there were between 40 and 50 different tribes in South Carolina when the Europeans arrived. Some historians think that the total population of the area was 20,000 Native Americans, but this number is probably quite low. Many of the tribes in the area did not have many people in them. Some tribes had been in the area for centuries, while others had arrived recently. Native Americans lived throughout the state from the coast and lowlands up into the Appalachian Mountains.

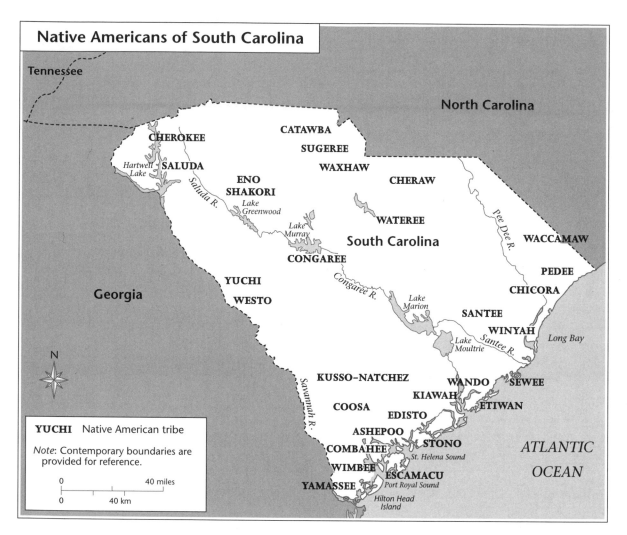

Native Americans of South Carolina

Tennessee

North Carolina

CHEROKEE

CATAWBA

SUGEREE

Hartwell Lake · SALUDA

WAXHAW

ENO SHAKORI

CHERAW

Saluda R.

Lake Greenwood

Lake Murray

WATEREE

South Carolina

Pee Dee R.

WACCAMAW

Georgia

CONGAREE

Congaree R.

PEDEE

YUCHI

CHICORA

WESTO

Lake Marion

SANTEE

WINYAH

Lake Moultrie

Santee R.

Long Bay

KUSSO–NATCHEZ

WANDO

SEWEE

Savannah R.

KIAWAH

COOSA

EDISTO

ETIWAN

ASHEPOO

STONO

COMBAHEE

St. Helena Sound

ATLANTIC OCEAN

WIMBEE

ESCAMACU

Port Royal Sound

YAMASSEE

Hilton Head Island

N

YUCHI Native American tribe

Note: Contemporary boundaries are provided for reference.

0   40 miles

0   40 km

The map shows some of the many tribes that were present in South Carolina before Europeans began to settle there.

Ethnographers and anthropologists divide Native Americans into groups based on the languages they spoke. The Native American languages are divided into approximately 60 different family groups. Within each group, there were often numerous dialects. The tribes of South Carolina spoke languages that belong to at least four of these groups. The largest tribe in the area, the Cherokee, lived in the mountains of the Carolinas, Virginia, Alabama, Georgia, and Tennessee, and spoke three different dialects of the

Iroquoian language family. The Catawba, who were the second largest tribe, lived in central South Carolina. They spoke a language from the Siouan group. The Westo and Yamasee lived along the Savannah River and spoke a language that belonged to the Muskogean group. A number of other tribes spoke languages related to the Algonquian languages spoken by the Native Americans in the Northeast.

Many of the smaller tribes, especially those along the coast, quickly disappeared as Europeans began to settle in South Carolina. Disease and warfare wiped out many of them. Other groups were taken away to be sold as slaves by the Europeans. Many who survived joined other tribes. By the middle of the 18th century, there were almost no Native Americans between the coast and the mountains in South Carolina.

THE CULTURE OF THE NATIVE AMERICANS IN SOUTH CAROLINA

There were many similarities among the various groups of Native Americans in South Carolina in the way they lived and how they thought about the world. The culture of a group of people is dictated in large part by the geography of the place where they live and by the technology they possess. The Native Americans of the area lived on the crops they grew and supplemented their diets with meat from wild animals. They also gathered many wild plants and fished in many of the area's streams, rivers, and lakes.

For the most part, the Native Americans lived in villages with their fields nearby. Villages ranged in size from a few families to

A participant in the French and Indian War, Austenaco was a Cherokee chief during the late 18th century. *(Library of Congress, Prints and Photographs Division [LC-USZ62-90958])*

Native Americans and Disease

Most scholars agree that the ancestors of the Native Americans originated in Asia and traveled to North America when the two continents were connected by a land bridge between modern-day Siberia and Alaska. During the thousands of years they were isolated from the Asian and European continents, they lost or never developed any immunity to the diseases that the Europeans brought with them to North America.

Common diseases for Europeans such as mumps and measles were often fatal to Native Americans. The most deadly disease, which had also killed large numbers of people in Europe, was smallpox. Smallpox epidemics ran through the Native American population of South Carolina numerous times during the colonial period. Very few Native Americans survived smallpox. In addition to European diseases, two other deadly diseases, yellow fever and malaria, plagued both the non-Indians and Native Americans of South Carolina.

Yellow fever and malaria are diseases that are spread by mosquitoes. They originated in Africa and arrived in the Americas via the slave trade. The swamps of South Carolina became breeding grounds for disease-carrying insects that infected people of all races. Many Europeans and even more Native Americans died from these diseases.

larger villages with over 500 dwellings. Some of the villages were seasonal. A group would move to the coast for the spring fishing. In the fall and early winter, they might move out to a hunting camp. Their main village would be along one of the many rivers where they would spend the summer tending their fields.

The east coast of North America was heavily wooded, and the Native Americans were very dependent on the forest. Their houses were built with a frame of saplings, small trees that could be bent to form a domed roof. The frame was then covered with large sheets of bark from trees. Inside, there would be woven mats made from grasses or palmetto fronds.

Many of the items they used in their daily lives were also made from wood. Bowls, spoons, weapons, and boats were all made from wood. They sometimes built wooden walls, known as palisades, around their villages to protect themselves from attack by raiding groups from other tribes. Conflicts between Native American groups prior to the coming of Europeans tended to be sporadic and

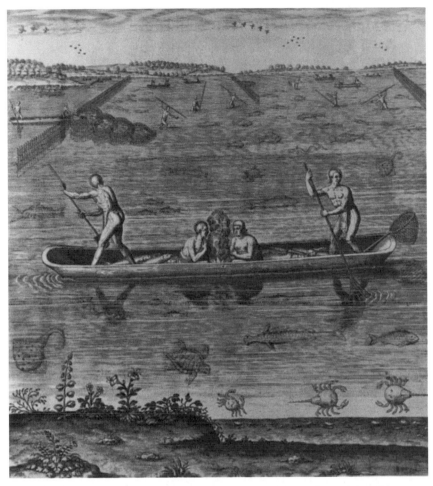

In this 1590s engraving by Thomas De Bry, American Indians along the east coast of the United States fish and prepare traps. *(Library of Congress, Prints and Photographs Division [LC-USZ62-576])*

on a small scale. Wars like those fought in Europe were unknown among the Native Americans. The small conflicts tended to be fought over territory or were carried out in revenge for acts committed in the past. The fact that the continent was so large and sparsely populated probably played a large part in the fact that most Native Americans got along with each other.

Game was plentiful, and most of the time their farming provided adequate food supplies. It has been estimated that 60 percent of the region's food came from farming. Most of the farming was done by Native American women. The primary crops they grew

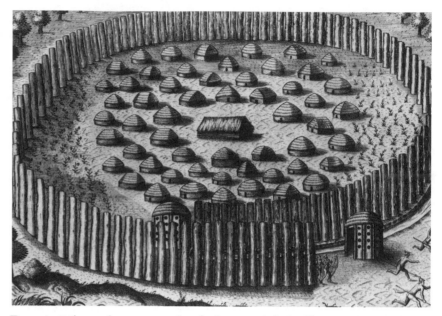

To protect themselves, some tribes built around their villages palisades (also called stockades), or a perimeter, made of tall timbers, sharpened at one end and driven into the ground. *(Library of Congress)*

Corn

Corn is an indigenous American crop that was developed in Central America about 5,000 years ago. It was propagated from a wild grass. Over time, the practice of raising corn spread throughout North and South America. Evidence of corn in the Southeast goes back approximately 3,000 years.

The Cherokee and the other Native Americans of the area grew three types of corn. One type was eaten fresh like the corn on the cob that is still popular today. Another type of corn was dried and later ground into cornmeal or added to stews and other dishes. The final type was a corn that could be roasted and then eaten later, like the corn nuts that are available as a snack food today.

Corn and beans were planted together. When grown together, the two plants help each other. The cornstalks provide a support for the bean vines, while the beans help replace the nitrogen that the corn takes out of the soil. When combined in foods, beans and corn complement each other as well. Together, they make a source of complete protein that enhanced the Native Americans' diet.

As one of the American Indian tribes in what is now the southeastern United States, the Timucua depended on farming for much of their food. This engraving of a painting by Jacques Le Moyne, a founder of the Huguenot colony at Fort Caroline near the mouth of the St. Johns River in Florida in the mid-16th century, demonstrates a European influence on the Timucua's planting of crops. *(Library of Congress, Prints and Photographs Division [LC-DIG-ppmsca-02937])*

were corn, beans, and squash. They also grew sunflowers and tobacco. Tobacco was smoked on ceremonial occasions as a way of helping send prayers up to the spirit world.

One of the most important celebrations for the Native Americans in South Carolina was known as the Green Corn Dance. This occurred each year when the first corn of the season was ready to eat. The celebration was one of thanks because the season's crops were thriving. In addition to the Green Corn Dance, the Native Americans had a very rich spiritual life. The spirit world they believed in was inhabited by many beings, some of whom were more important than others.

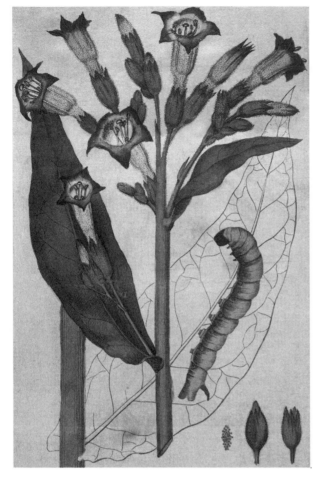

American Indians cultivated tobacco, shown in this 18th-century illustration, throughout the Americas. *(National Archives of Canada)*

Many early Christian observers tried to make the Native American religious beliefs fit into their own way of thinking. Early accounts by Europeans on Native American beliefs tend to focus on a Great Spirit who ruled over the heavens and an Evil Spirit who ruled over the underworld. The relationship between Native Americans and the spirit world was more complicated than that. The animals, trees, rivers, and land were all connected to the spirit world, and it was the role of the people to try and live in harmony with it.

When crops were successful, thanks were given to the corn spirit and the bean spirit. When a tree was cut down, it was done with respect for the spirits of the forest. A successful hunt happened because the spirit of the deer allowed the hunter to kill it. Children were never hit or made to cry because people believed the spirits would think the parent did not want the child and would come take the child away. Failure to understand the beliefs of Native Americans was one of the reasons that Europeans never succeeded in appreciating the people they found in America.

The Native Americans of South Carolina, like others throughout the continent, had no written language and preserved their history and religion through storytellers. They had no formal schools. Children were taught their role and responsibilities by helping the adults. Boys were instructed by their uncles, while the girls often spent time with their maternal aunts and grandmother. They also listened to the storytellers to learn about their history and religion.

All Native Americans have a story in their oral tradition that tells how they believe the world was created. Many of the stories are very similar. The Cherokee creation story has been recorded and is a good example. The Cherokee believe that the world was originally covered by water and all living things lived above the sky in a place called Galun'lati. As this place became crowded, the people and animals there began to wonder if they could somehow live in the water world below the sky.

It was decided to send a water beetle down to look for a place they could go. All the water beetle found was ocean. The beetle decided to look under the water and dove down to the bottom. It brought up some mud. When the beetle released the mud, it began to expand until it grew into a flat, soft plain. After the water beetle returned to tell what happened, birds were sent to see if they could move to the land.

The land was very flat, and when they landed, they sank into the mud. Everyone was very discouraged, and they waited a long time before they checked the earth again. This time they sent down the great buzzard to fly over the still-soft ground. As it flew low,

In this early 17th-century drawing by Samuel de Champlain, an American Indian deer hunt is in progress. Some American Indians startle the deer into running toward traps depicted on the right side of the image. *(National Archives of Canada)*

Deer

Although the Native Americans in South Carolina hunted and ate just about every type of animal from squirrels to alligators, the white-tailed deer was their primary quarry. More than half the meat they ate came from deer. They also used most of the rest of the deer. Hides were used for clothing. Bones and antlers were made into tools. The tough tissue that connects muscles to bones, known as sinew, was used as string. Even the brains were used in the tanning process for the hides.

The men were the hunters, and they used a variety of ways to hunt deer. Many deer were stalked by hunters wearing deerskins so they could get close enough to shoot a deer with a bow and arrow. At other times, large groups would hunt together and drive the deer into an enclosure where they could be easily shot with an arrow or speared.

When the Europeans first arrived in South Carolina, they were amazed at the parklike nature of much of the forest. The Native Americans would regularly burn the understory of the forest to encourage the growth of grass for the deer to graze on. Once the hunters got rifles from the Europeans, they began to harvest deer in large numbers. In 1748, Native Americans supplied 160,000 deer hides, which were shipped out of Charleston to be sold in Europe, where leather pants were very popular. It has been estimated that several million deer hides were shipped out of South Carolina during colonial times.

American Indians used almost every part of the white-tailed deer that they killed. *(National Park Service)*

This photograph of the Blue Ridge Mountains taken from the Blue Ridge Parkway in North Carolina makes clear the valleys and ridges mentioned in the Cherokee creation story. *(National Park Service)*

the power of its wings caused the flat land to form into valleys and ridges. This created the mountain homelands of the Cherokee.

The rich beliefs of the Cherokee and the other Native Americans were almost wiped out by the Europeans, who brought disease, captured them to become slaves, and forced them off their traditional lands. By the time the colonies became the United States, there were almost no Native Americans in South Carolina.

3

The Coming of the English

In 1588, the power of Spain to control the oceans of the world ended with the defeat of the Spanish Armada by the English. It was at this time that English interest in the land they claimed in North America began to grow. However, early settlements by the English took root in New England and Virginia while the land between Florida and Virginia was still inhabited only by Native Americans and a handful of pirates who hid along the coast.

In 1629, Charles I, king of England, granted all the land in North America between 31° and 36° north latitude to Sir Robert Heath, the attorney general of England at the time. At first, Heath talked to a group of French Huguenots, who had fled to England during the French civil war, about a colony in what the English also called Carolana. In 1633, 40 colonists headed for America to settle in Carolana. However, they stopped in Virginia and decided to stay there rather than move farther south into the wilderness of Carolana.

Heath grew disenchanted with the idea of colonizing Carolana and gave up his grant to Henry, Lord Maltravers. In the 1630s, Lord Maltravers was no more successful at colony building than Heath. Poor planning, lack of money, and bad timing left Carolana empty of Europeans for another 30 years.

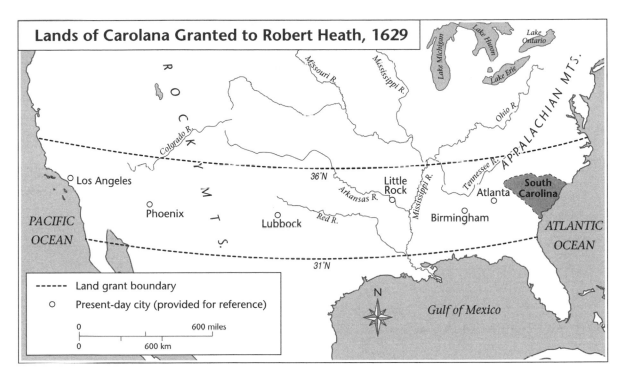

Lands of Carolana Granted to Robert Heath, 1629

Land grant boundary
Present-day city (provided for reference)

600 miles

600 km

The original English charter included all the land between 31° and 36° north latitude, and went from the Atlantic Ocean to the Pacific Ocean.

SETTING UP THE PROPRIETARY COLONY OF CAROLINA

Charles I of England had numerous problems during his reign and was overthrown in 1649 by a Puritan revolt. He was executed by Oliver Cromwell and his Puritan followers. Cromwell ruled England for the next 10 years. After Cromwell's death, the monarchy was restored in England. Charles I's son became King Charles II on May 8, 1660. Many of those who had helped Charles II regain the throne were rewarded with positions in his government, and a select few were given large tracts of land in North America.

On March 24, 1663, Charles II signed the Charter of Carolina, which granted the lands that Charles I had given to Sir Robert Heath to a new group. These eight men were the owners or proprietors of the colony, and the charter stated what rights they had

A Description of Carolina from the Original Charter

. . . all that territory or tract of ground, scituate, lying and being within our dominions of America, extending from the north end of the island called Lucke island, which lieth in the southern Virginia seas, and within six and thirty degrees of the northern latitude, and to the west as far as the south seas, and so southerly as far as the river St. Matthias, which bordereth upon the coast of Florida, and within one and thirty degrees of northern latitude, and so west in a direct line as far as the south seas aforesaid; together with all and singular ports, harbours, bays, rivers, isles and islets belonging to the country aforesaid; and also all the soil, lands, fields, woods, mounthills, fields, lakes, rivers, bays and islets, scituate or being within the bounds or limits aforesaid, with the fishing of all sorts of fish, whales, sturgeons and all other royal fishes in the sea, bays, islets and rivers within the premises, and the fish therein taken; and moreover all veins, mines, quarries, as well discovered as not discovered, of gold, silver, gems, precious stones, and all other whatsoever, be it of stones, metals, or any other thing whatsoever, found or to be found within the countries, isles and limits aforesaid.

and described the boundaries of their land. It was at this time that the name of the areas was changed from Carolana to Carolina.

The new proprietors of Carolina were Edward, earl of Clarendon; George Monk, first duke of Albemarle; William Lord Craven; John Lord Berkley; Anthony Lord Ashley; Sir George Carteret; Sir William Berkley; and Sir John Colleton. These men were granted absolute power to create whatever type of colony they wanted. Within the charter was the right to levy taxes, raise and maintain an army, and all the other rights involved in running a government.

Charles II ruled England, Scotland, and Ireland from 1660 until his death in 1685. *(Library of Congress, Prints and Photographs Division [LC-USZ62-96910])*

However, these men understood that to compete with the existing colonies in North America, they would have to grant many rights to the colonists. To do this, a constitution was needed. Lord Ashley, born Anthony Ashley Cooper and later known as the first earl of Shaftesbury, was the proprietor who took the most active role in trying to develop the colony of Carolina. With the help of his friend and physician, John Locke, Cooper wrote the Fundamental Constitutions of Carolina in 1669. Locke was one of the most influential philosophers of his time, and his writings on political thought had a profound impact on those in the colonies.

The Fundamental Constitutions has 128 articles that outline the structure of the Carolina colony. The colony was to be carefully divided into counties. Then, according to article three, "each county shall consist of eight seigniories, eight baronies, and four precincts; each precinct shall consist of six colonies." Locke and Cooper wanted to create a colony with an upper class of landowners. Members of the "Grand Council" needed to have at least 500 acres, whereas to vote in elections people needed to own a minimum of 50 acres.

George Monk, first duke of Albermarle, was one of the original eight proprietors of Carolina. *(Library of Congress, Prints and Photographs Division [LC-USZ62-85339])*

A large section of the Fundamental Constitutions outlines a complex legal system that was designed to protect the rights of anyone who moved to Carolina. It guaranteed a trial by jury and other aspects of the English legal system. It was important to assure potential colonists that they would receive the "basic rights of Englishmen" if they came to the colony. One hundred years later, it would be an infringement on the "basic rights" of the colonists that would lead to the War for Independence.

In addition to setting up the structure of the colony and a legal system, the Fundamental Constitutions offered potential settlers religious freedom. This was important because religious persecution was a serious problem in Europe and in some of the other colonies. Only Rhode Island was said to be more liberal in its tolerance of a wide variety of religious groups.

John Locke
(1632–1704)

John Locke was a physician and philosopher who had a profound impact on the thinking of modern society. His theory that humans learned from their experiences changed the way many people looked at the world. He is given credit for much of what is included in the Fundamental Constitutions. His writings about government were taken to heart by those who wanted the American colonies to be free from the arbitrary rule of the Crown. The following section from chapter 7 of his *The Second Treatise on Government*, written in 1690, are echoed later in the Declaration of Independence and the U.S. Constitution:

Man being born, as has been proved, with a title to perfect freedom and an uncontrolled enjoyment of all the rights and privileges of the law of Nature, equally with any other man, or number of men in the world, hath by nature a power not only to preserve his property—that is, his life, liberty, and estate—against the injuries and attempts of other men, but to judge of and punish the breaches of that law in others, as he is persuaded the offence deserves, even with death itself, in crimes where the heinousness of the fact, in his opinion, requires it.

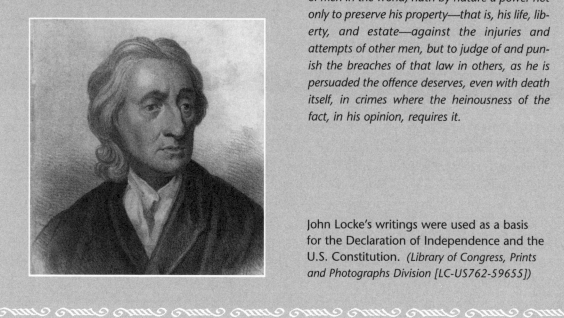

John Locke's writings were used as a basis for the Declaration of Independence and the U.S. Constitution. *(Library of Congress, Prints and Photographs Division [LC-US762-59655])*

Despite the forward-thinking nature of the Fundamental Constitutions, it also guaranteed that the absolute rights of slave owners over their slaves would be protected. The proprietors hoped to attract colonists from the West Indies to Carolina. In the

islands, large plantations that used slaves for labor had become the accepted practice and would become an important part of the colony and state of South Carolina.

The generous provisions of the Fundamental Constitutions were not enough to start a rush of colonists to Carolina. Many religious dissenters already had colonies they could join in America. The Puritans had settled New England, Quakers were in New Jersey and would soon have Pennsylvania as their own colony, and Catholics were going to Maryland. The proprietors of Carolina would have to offer more than a progressive constitution to attract people. In April 1669, Cooper convinced his fellow proprietors to each put up £500. The money was used to recruit and finance the first settlement of 100 colonists.

<table>
<tr><td>

Article 101 of the Fundamental Constitutions

"No person whatsoever shall disturb, molest, or persecute another for his speculative opinions in religion, or his way of worship."

</td></tr>
</table>

THE FIRST ENGLISH SETTLERS

The eight proprietors of Carolina put together an expedition of three ships, the *Carolina*, the *Albemarle*, and the *Port Royal*, under the command of Captain Joseph West. They loaded the ships with 100 colonists and all the supplies they would need to start a colony. The ships stopped in Ireland and Barbados in hopes of picking up more colonists. However, in Ireland they actually lost people because some of the colonists left the ships. If they thought the passage from England to Ireland had been too rough, they would not have been able to imagine what lay ahead for the remaining colonists.

The passage from Ireland to Barbados went well, and they arrived there in November. Then there were a series of disasters. First, a late-season storm blew into Barbados and the *Albemarle* sank. Captain West continued on with the *Port Royal*, the *Carolina*, and a ship leased in Barbados. As the three ships sailed from Barbados to Carolina, another storm hit them. The leased ship was blown so far off course that it ended up in Virginia. Then the *Port Royal* was shipwrecked in the Bahamas. Finally, on March 15, 1670, the *Carolina* arrived in the colony that shared its name.

It had been the plan of the proprietors that the colony be established at Port Royal near the sites of the earlier French and Spanish forts. William Sayle, an 80-year-old former government official in Bermuda, had been appointed governor by the colonists from Barbados, and some of the other leaders decided

that Port Royal was too close to the Spanish settlements in Florida and what would become Georgia. So, instead of staying at Port Royal, they sailed 50 miles up the coast to the river the Native Americans called the Kiawah but the settlers called the Ashley.

On the Ashley River, the colonists established the community of Albemarle Point. The name was soon changed to Charles Towne in honor of the king. In 1680, they moved the town to a better location on the point of land between the Ashley and Cooper Rivers. Then in 1783, the name of the town was shortened to Charleston, which it remains today.

The grand designs of the Fundamental Constitutions were put on hold, and a temporary government with a governor, deputies appointed by the proprietors, and five elected freemen was established. The proprietors also set up a temporary parliament that

This detail from a 1682 map by Joel Gascoyne shows the area in and around Charles Towne, later shortened to Charleston. Originally located on a low, swampy point along the Ashley River, Charleston was moved to more elevated land between the Ashley and Cooper Rivers. *(Library of Congress)*

included 20 elected members. This temporary government caused as many problems as it solved. There were disagreements over the legality of the elections and land distribution. The fact that Governor Sayle was 80 and becoming senile made the problems even worse.

There was a disagreement over who the next governor should be. The Barbadian Sir John Yeamans felt he was the highest ranking member of the colony and should be governor. Sayles had appointed Captain Joseph West to the job. The proprietors backed Yeamans, who became governor. Yet, he proved to be unpopular. At the time, there was a conflict between the settlers from England and those from Barbados. The Barbadians tended to be wealthier and better prepared for life in the colony. They were also more concerned about making money than they were about the welfare of their fellow colonists.

Governor Yeamans is reported to have sold the excess produce of his farm back to Barbados, where he could make more money than if he sold it in Carolina, where there was a food shortage. Fortunately for the colonists, Dr. Henry Woodward had spent time among the Native Americans of the area and was able to trade with them for food. Without Woodward's help, the English experience

Dr. Henry Woodward
(ca. 1646–ca. 1686)

Dr. Henry Woodward was a surgeon who was probably from Barbados. He moved to North Carolina when he was about 20. In June 1666, he set out with some other people to explore the lands to the south. Woodward was invited to live with a group of Native Americans along the South Carolina coast and became the first Englishman to live in South Carolina. When the Spanish heard about him, they became concerned that he might convince the Native Americans to attack their settlements in Florida. The Spanish went out and captured Woodward.

He was put in prison in St. Augustine but was released by an English privateer who attacked St. Augustine. Woodward then served as a ship's surgeon for a few years. In 1669, he joined the group that was headed to South Carolina to establish a colony. His experience living with the Native Americans along the coast turned into a valuable asset for the struggling colony.

Rice became a staple crop in early Carolina life along the moist coast. The rice fields in this 1910 photograph are located in Louisiana. *(Library of Congress, Prints and Photographs Division [LC-USZ62-51001])*

in Carolina might have been more like the disappointing attempts of the French and the Spanish to settle the area.

In addition to food shortages, the colonists soon learned that Carolina was not an easy place to survive. People from England found it very difficult to adjust to the heat and humidity of the area. Just as Native Americans had no immunity to European diseases, the Europeans became sick from the mosquito-borne diseases of malaria and yellow fever that had been brought to the colony by their African slaves. Many died. Overcoming these hardships was one of the major challenges for the settlers in Carolina. To solve these problems, the white property owners in Carolina did two things. First, they began importing more slaves, who would soon outnumber the free whites in the colony, and they began growing rice in the low country along the rivers and swamps of the coastline.

Despite difficulties colonists faced in Carolina, people continued to come to the colony from Barbados, England, and the other American colonies. By 1680, there were 1,000 whites, 200 African slaves, and an unknown number of Native American slaves in and around Charleston. Many in the colony ignored the laws of the proprietors. Carolina became a center for trade in Native America slaves. It also became a stopping place for the pirates who attacked the trade routes along the southeast coast and in the Caribbean.

In 1680, Charleston, which was still the only town in the colony, was moved to a better site. The original location had been on low ground near a swamp, and the colonists realized that was unhealthy. The new site was on higher ground, on a point of land between the Ashley and Cooper Rivers. It is where Charleston is today.

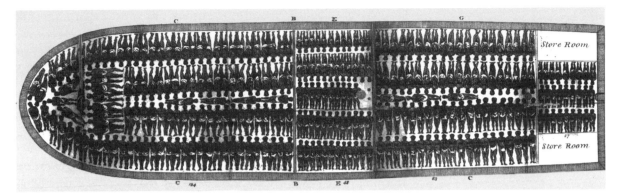

In this detail from a 1780s etching, captured Africans are crammed into the hold of a British slave ship, the *Brookes*, similar in design to many others used to transport slaves. *(Library of Congress, Prints and Photographs Division [LC-USZ62-44000])*

A group of 150 Scots arrived in 1683 and established Stuart Town on Port Royal Sound. This short-lived attempt at settlement suffered greatly from disease. Stuart Town was soon attacked by the Spanish, and the remaining settlers were wiped out. The next group to arrive in Charleston was made up of 500 Huguenots, who left France after the Edict of Nantes was revoked in 1681. There were also large numbers of English Presbyterians and Baptists who came to South Carolina to practice their religion without fear of persecution.

Edict of Nantes
(1598)

The Edict of Nantes ended a long period of civil war between the Protestant Huguenots and Catholics in France in 1598. It granted Huguenots the right to practice their religion and guaranteed them the same rights as all other French people. There were even special provisions to ensure the Huguenot minority would be represented in local and national assemblies.

When Cardinal Richelieu, the chief minister of the French king Louis XIII, started to ignore the edict, problems began again between Catholics and Huguenots. When Louis XIV repealed the Edict of Nantes in 1685, many Huguenots left France and headed to the Americas as they had done during the years of religious civil war in France.

The arrival of these dissenting religious groups created a number of problems in South Carolina. The majority of the early settlers, especially those from Barbados, were members of the Anglican Church, also known as the Church of England. They did not share the ideas of religious toleration expressed by the Fundamental Constitutions. Their religious bigotry caused numerous conflicts between themselves and the new arrivals.

Politics in the early years of South Carolina were also full of conflicts. As the proprietors' representative in the colony, the governor was frequently at odds with the people of the colony. Numerous governors came and went in South Carolina. Many of them were forced out of office because of the laws they tried to enact or because of disagreements they had with the other leaders of the colony. One governor, Seth Sothell, was kicked out of both North and South Carolina.

Seth Sothell

Seth Sothell had bought out Lord Clarendon's share of the Carolina grant, which made him one of the proprietors. He had been governor in North Carolina but was removed from office in 1690 by the assembly there for his illegal actions. When he arrived in Charleston, he landed in the middle of a fight between the governor and the most influential planters in South Carolina. The planters wanted Governor James Colleton out. They used the fact that Sothell was a proprietor, and therefore of higher rank than Colleton, to replace him with Sothell.

Unlike his tenure in North Carolina, Sothell seemed to get along with the planters in South Carolina. He gave their assembly the right to pass many laws during the time he was governor. Some of these laws were progressive for the time. Some have speculated that Sothell was just biding his time until he was in position to control the Native American trade.

Fortunately, he never got the chance. Instead of being thrown out by the assembly in South Carolina, his actions upset the other proprietors, and he was recalled to London. The new governor immediately repealed the laws that had been passed during Sothell's governorship. Although the laws were repealed, many South Carolinians came through the Sothell governorship believing they were entitled to rule themselves.

Some rice growers use houses such as this one (photographed in 1977) on the Chicora Wood Plantation in Georgetown County, South Carolina, to store rice after it is harvested and before it is exported. *(Library of Congress, Prints and Photographs Division [HABS, SC, 22-GEOTO.V, 7F])*

Despite conflicts, disease, and lawlessness, South Carolina prospered and grew. Charleston quickly became a major port, and rice became the colony's major export. One area of concern for the leaders of the colony was that there were soon more slaves in the colony than whites.

Life in Colonial South Carolina

Although North and South Carolina were originally thought of as one colony, they had very little in common. They were also separated by a great distance. Settlement in North Carolina was close to the Virginia border, while in South Carolina, people originally settled in the southeast corner. The first settlers in North Carolina mostly came from Virginia and started small farms, while the people in South Carolina came from the Caribbean islands and England and established large plantations. There were also separate administrations for the two Carolinas.

In 1712, the division that existed between the southern and northern parts of Carolina became official as North and South Carolina became separate colonies. As South Carolina began to prosper, it was also apparent that its existence was precarious. Native Americans, pirates, slave rebellions, the French, and the Spanish all presented threats to the existence of the colony. Disease was another problem that was always present in the low country of South Carolina.

RELATIONS WITH THE NATIVE AMERICANS OF SOUTH CAROLINA

From the very beginning of the colony, the Europeans exploited the Native Americans in South Carolina. One of the first sources of profit for the colonists was trading with Native Americans for

The Diseases Faced by the Colonists in South Carolina

The healthy climate of North America presented very few threats to the colonists. They also had a certain amount of immunity to the diseases that they brought with them that wiped out so many Native Americans. It was two diseases brought from Africa by slaves that threatened the colonists in South Carolina.

Yellow fever and malaria are both blood-borne diseases that are transmitted from one human being to another by mosquitoes. Yellow fever is a virus that attacks the blood and the liver. As the liver becomes overloaded from the disease, it cannot process the bile that it usually eliminates, and the afflicted person turns yellow. There is still no known treatment for yellow fever, and it often kills within four to eight days. Today, a vaccine exists to prevent it. In colonial times, those who survived yellow fever became immune and never got it again.

Malaria is actually a single-cell parasite that feeds on the red blood cells in the body. The parasites are born in the host mosquitoes, which then transmit them to humans. The disease causes high fever combined with shaking and chills. In severe cases it is fatal. Approximately 300 million to 500 million people a year still contract malaria. As many as 2.5 million people still die each year from the disease. Controlling mosquitoes in North America has almost eliminated the disease in the United States.

deerskins that were a valuable commodity in Europe. Deerskin was used to make articles of clothing, especially leather pants, which were in style at the time.

By the end of the colonial period, South Carolina traders were getting deer hides from as far west as the Mississippi River and even beyond. There were numerous attempts by the proprietors and the Crown to control and profit from the trade. For the most part, the people in South Carolina ignored all attempts to regulate the trade in deer hides. The profits were too great for them to give it up.

The other trade with Native Americans is one that is often neglected in the discussion of the state's history. It has been estimated that at one time during the colonial period, there were as many as 1,500 Native American slaves working in the fields of South Carolina. In addition to that, South Carolina slave traders shipped as many as 10,000 Native Americans to the slave markets of the

Caribbean. To do this, the people involved in the slave trade pitted one Native American group against another. The captives in the conflicts between tribes were traded to the white slave traders and then exported.

The mistreatment of Native Americans became an even more serious problem when the Tuscarora in North Carolina decided to fight back. In September 1711, the Tuscarora attacked New Bern, North Carolina, and killed around 140 colonists. South Carolina came to the aid of its sister colony by putting together a small force of colonists and more than 1,000 Native Americans, most of whom were Yamasee. The colonists' treatment of their Native American allies was so inhumane that shortly after the Tuscarora War, the Yamasee started their own war in South Carolina.

On April 15, 1715, the Yamasee attacked the area around Beaufort. They killed more than 100 settlers in their initial attack. During the next two years, more than 400 of the colony's 1,200 men able to bear arms against the Yamasee were killed in battle. Most people abandoned their plantations and fled to Charleston. At the height of the Yamasee War, the colony was reduced to the lands within 30 miles of Charleston.

If the Yamasee War had lasted much longer, the colony of South Carolina might have come to an end. However, the colonists were able to negotiate a peace treaty with the Yamasee in 1717 to end the war. In Charleston, the situation was difficult. No crops had been planted during the war. There were food shortages, and with one out of every three able-bodied men lost in the war, it was difficult to reclaim what had been lost.

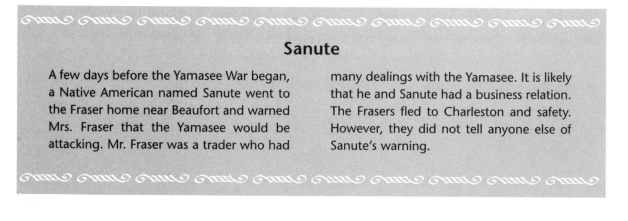

Sanute

A few days before the Yamasee War began, a Native American named Sanute went to the Fraser home near Beaufort and warned Mrs. Fraser that the Yamasee would be attacking. Mr. Fraser was a trader who had many dealings with the Yamasee. It is likely that he and Sanute had a business relation. The Frasers fled to Charleston and safety. However, they did not tell anyone else of Sanute's warning.

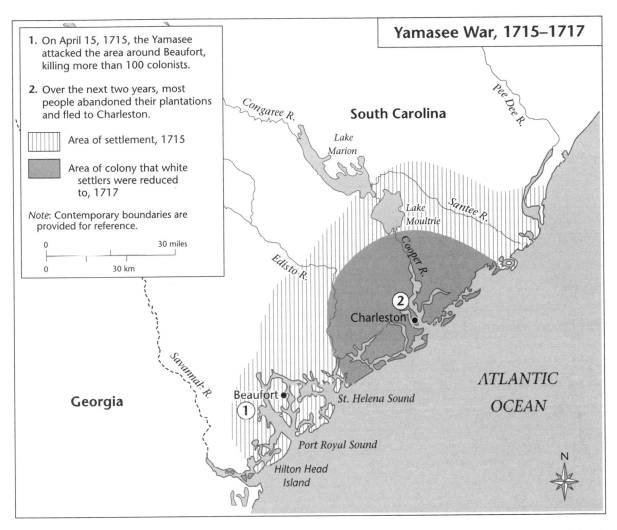

1. On April 15, 1715, the Yamasee attacked the area around Beaufort, killing more than 100 colonists.

2. Over the next two years, most people abandoned their plantations and fled to Charleston.

||||| Area of settlement, 1715

▨ Area of colony that white settlers were reduced to, 1717

Note: Contemporary boundaries are provided for reference.

0   30 miles

0   30 km

During the Yamasee War, which started near Beaufort, South Carolina, the colonists were only able to defend the land within 30 miles of Charleston.

PIRATES AND SOUTH CAROLINA

When the colony of South Carolina was first started, many of the colonists were friendly with the pirates who preyed on the ships that passed the coast. The pirates sold their captured booty cheaply. They also paid in gold and silver coins for the supplies they bought from the colonists. Money was always hard to come by in the American colonies, and it was difficult to turn away customers who paid in cash.

Blackbeard
(ca. 1680–1718)

Edward Teach, who was known by the nickname Blackbeard, may have been one of the most savage pirates in America. He reportedly would cut off a captive's finger if he or she refused to give up a ring that he wanted. He started his career as a privateer in the employ of the English. When Queen Anne's War ended in 1713, he continued to attack shipping as a pirate.

He is reported to have said, "Come let us make a Hell of [our] own, and try how long we can bear it."

Apparently, it was not very long. Although he was granted a pardon by the governor of North Carolina in January 1718, he continued to terrorize shipping along the coast. After his attack on Charleston, his reign of terror came to an end when he was killed by a force from Virginia.

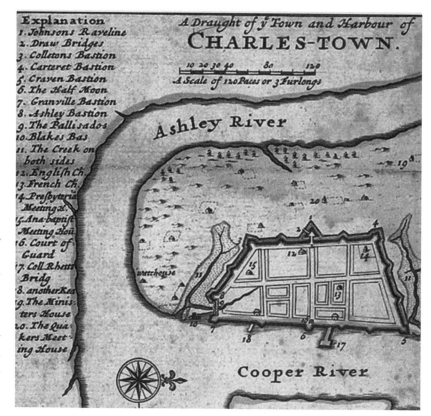

This detail of a 1715 map by Herman Moll focuses on Charles Towne's main settlement, especially the harbor, between the Ashley and Cooper Rivers. The complicated figure on the Cooper River side of the settlement represents the large fort the town contained.
(Library of Congress)

However, as the colony grew, its attitude toward pirates began to change. When the South Carolina merchants and plantation owners started shipping goods out of the colony, they, too, became the victims of pirates. By 1700, the officials in Charleston began to fight back, and numerous pirates were captured and executed.

If anyone was still sympathetic to pirates, they probably changed their feelings in 1718. One of the most feared pirates of the time was Edward Teach, who was called "Blackbeard." In 1718, he attacked the shipping of Charleston right in the mouth of the harbor, capturing ships and holding the passengers hostage. After he escaped from Charleston, Blackbeard was captured and killed. The 14 pirates who survived the battle were tried and hanged.

Later that same year, another famous pirate, Stede Bonnet, was hunted down and captured by a force from South Carolina. Bonnet was called the "gentleman pirate" and apparently still had some sympathizers in Charleston. With outside help, he managed to escape from Charleston wearing women's clothing. He was quickly recaptured. During November and December 1718, Bonnet and approximately 50 of his followers were tried and hung in Charleston. The pirates who were wounded were tried and executed first so as not to cheat the hangman by dying of their injuries first.

Stede Bonnet
(unknown–1718)

Stede Bonnet was born into a wealthy family, served as a major in the British army, and had a plantation on the island of Barbados. In 1717, he had apparently become bored with his life on the plantation. He decided to become a pirate and bought a sloop that he named *Revenge*. He may have hoped to be commissioned as a privateer, but when that did not happen, he and his crew turned to piracy. Because of his upbringing, he was known as the "gentleman pirate." Bonnet often collaborated with Blackbeard. Yet at one point, Blackbeard held Bonnet prisoner.

Bonnet and his crew successfully captured a number of ships off the coast of Virginia and in Delaware Bay. He was captured hiding out in the Cape Fear River in North Carolina before he was brought to Charleston for trial and execution.

SOUTH CAROLINA AND SLAVES

When the white plantation owners in South Carolina were not fighting Native Americans, pirates, or disease, they were becoming some of the richest people in the colonies. Their wealth came from the labor of the slaves they owned. By 1720, it is estimated that there were just over 17,000 people in South Carolina. Seventy percent, or approximately 12,000, of them were slaves of African

Probably dating back to the 1780s, this newspaper advertisement announces that 250 slaves will be sold at Ashley Ferry near Charleston. *(Library of Congress, Prints and Photographs Division [LC-USZ62-10293])*

Built around the 1840s, this one-room cabin, typical of many slave quarters except for its Gothic details such as the arched door and window frames, is one of several such cabins located on Arundel Plantation, a mid-19th century rice plantation in Georgetown County, South Carolina. *(Library of Congress, Prints and Photographs Division [HARS, SC, 22 GEOTO.V, 11A-8])*

descent. The most successful plantation owners had multiple plantations with thousands of acres. Their homes were furnished with goods from England. Their children were often sent to England for school or had private tutors. Many were members of the Anglican Church and attended church every Sunday. However, as the planters and their families prospered, slaves worked long hours in their fields and homes, lived in poor housing, and were barely given enough food to survive.

Many of the slaves in South Carolina in the early years of the colony came from the Caribbean and were given responsibilities as cowherds, boatmen, and farmers. However, as rice became the primary crop of the plantations, more and more slaves were brought directly from Africa. Many of them came from the part of Africa that is now Angola. The majority of the Africans were young men. No one ever willingly became a slave.

The Spanish in Florida let it be known that they would give freedom to any slave who ran away and came to St. Augustine. It

In this early 20th-century photograph, African Americans hoe rice on a plantation in South Carolina in much the same way as it had been done in the days of slavery. *(Library of Congress, Prints and Photographs Division [LC-USZ62-26232])*

is estimated that about 1 percent of the slaves in South Carolina were able to escape. However, on Sunday, September 9, 1739, approximately 20 slaves who had gathered at Hutchenson's Store near the Stono River, in St. Paul's Parish southwest of Charleston, decided as a group to go to Florida. This is known as the Stono Rebellion.

According to some accounts, the leader of the group of slaves was known as Jemmy. He and about 20 other slaves started the rebellion. They killed and beheaded the two storekeepers and then stole a number of weapons. They then marched south toward Florida, beating drums and yelling "liberty." It is esti-

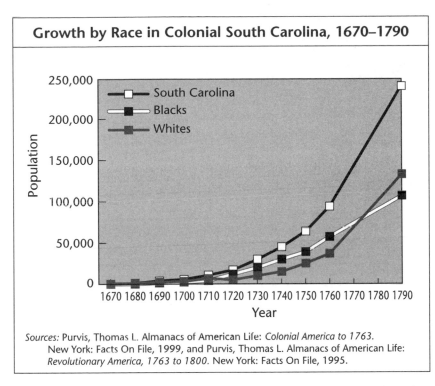

Growth by Race in Colonial South Carolina, 1670–1790

Sources: Purvis, Thomas L. *Almanacs of American Life: Colonial America to 1763.* New York: Facts On File, 1999, and Purvis, Thomas L. *Almanacs of American Life: Revolutionary America, 1763 to 1800.* New York: Facts On File, 1995.

For much of the colonial period, there were more African-American slaves in South Carolina than there were whites.

mated that as many as 80 more slaves joined the rebellion. As they headed for freedom in Florida, they attacked and burned several plantations, killing more than 20 white people along the way.

Because the rebellion took place on a Sunday, most of the plantation owners were at church and unarmed when the rebellion started. By the time Lieutenant Governor William Bull was able to raise the militia and catch up with the slaves, they were within 50 miles of the Florida border. The whites showed no mercy. All the participants in the Stono Rebellion who were captured were shot or hanged. Many of those who were hanged were left hanging for some time after their death as a warning to the other slaves that there would be no toleration of rebellion.

For a time after the Stono Rebellion, any slave who was even suspected of considering rebellion was executed. Some historians

Located on Green Hill Plantation in Virginia, these two stone structures are believed to have been used to auction slaves. The auctioneer stood on the smaller slab while slaves stood on the larger auction block for the buyers to inspect. *(Library of Congress, Prints and Photographs Division [HABS, VA, 16-LONI.V, 1J-2])*

believe that had the participants in the Stono Rebellion reached Florida, there might have been a general uprising among the slaves in South Carolina. To ensure that there would not be any further rebellions in South Carolina, in 1740 the legislature passed the strictest Slave Code in the colonies, tried to cut back on the number of new slaves brought in from Africa, and passed a law that white men had to bring their weapons to church on Sundays.

The plantation economy flourished, and soon added another cash crop. At the time, fabric for clothes was dyed using plants. Blue dye came from a plant called indigo that the British imported from Spain and France. It was expensive and hard to get when England was at war in Europe. By 1744, Eliza Lucas Pinckney, who was 22 at the time, had figured out how to grow indigo in South Carolina. It soon became the second cash crop of

The Slave Code of 1740

After the Stono Rebellion, the legislature of South Carolina passed a list of laws that were intended to prevent future rebellions among the slaves in the colony. The Slave Code of 1740 limited the number of hours that a slave could be made to work to 15 hours a day. It also allowed for slaves to have Sundays off.

To prevent illegal gatherings of slaves, any group of more than seven slaves traveling together needed their owner or overseer with them. All slaves were supposed to have a written pass if they left their plantation. The Slave Code also contained other rules about providing adequate food and clothing for slaves. It made it a crime for a white to kill a slave. Some in England felt that whites should be executed for killing slaves. However, the Slave Code called for a fine instead. The Slave Code remained in effect until the mid-1860s, when slavery was ended by the Emancipation Proclamation and constitutional amendments resulting from the Civil War.

Since indigo became a profitable crop in South Carolina during the mid-18th century, many colonists used slave labor to complete the complicated manufacturing process, shown in this undated illustration. *(Library of Congress, Prints and Photographs Division [LC-USZ62-53584])*

Elizabeth Lucas Pinckney
(1722–1793)

Eliza Pinckney, as she was known, was a remarkable woman. She was born on the Caribbean island of Antigua and was educated in England. Very few young men in the colonies were sent to England for schooling. The number of young women was much smaller. In addition to her accomplishments as a horticulturist, she ran her father's three plantations in South Carolina when he was called back to Antigua, where he served as royal governor. Later, after the death of her husband, she once again successfully ran the family plantations. To raise profits for her plantations, she tried to raise a number of cash crops including alfalfa, cotton, and ginger. It was her experiments with growing indigo that were the most successful.

When Eliza was 22, she married Charles Pinckney, who had been recently widowed. Eliza took an active interest in the education of her children and had her oldest son reading by the time he was two. Eliza also held school for the slaves on her plantation. She and her husband had three children who survived to adulthood. Her two sons grew up to be leaders in South Carolina and beyond.

Eliza's oldest son, Charles Cotesworth Pinckney, served in the Revolutionary War and became one of George Washington's aides. Charles was a delegate to the Constitutional Convention and played an active role in shaping the debate about the makeup of our federal government. Charles unsuccessfully ran for president twice.

His younger brother, Thomas, was also active in the Revolution and in state and federal politics. Thomas served two terms as governor of South Carolina. He also was responsible for negotiating the Pinckney Treaty with Spain in 1795. The treaty gave the United States the right to use the Mississippi River for shipping goods out of the Midwest, which was being settled at the time. Her daughter Harriot married Daniel Horry, a plantation owner.

South Carolina after rice. Shortly after Pinckney proved it could be grown in South Carolina, the colony was exporting more than 100,000 pounds of the dye a year.

The Slave Code prevented further uprisings among the slaves in South Carolina. However, the Spanish used the growing free black colony at Fort Mose in northern Florida to harass the border lands between Florida and the English colonies to the north.

RELATIONS WITH THE FRENCH AND SPANISH

Although the Spanish had been forced to abandon their settlements in South Carolina and Georgia, they did not give up their claim to the area. During the early years of the colony, there was a constant threat that the Spanish might sail north at any time and try to take back South Carolina. To protect South Carolina, it was decided one more English colony in North America. In February 1733, 114 colonists led by General James Oglethorpe landed at the site of Savannah, Georgia, and began a new experiment in colonization. Georgia was settled by people from the debtors' prisons of England. It was the only colony that was funded by Parliament in England.

In 1739, 400 South Carolina militiamen joined General Oglethorpe in an attack on St. Augustine. With the aid of British warships, Oglethorpe and his South Carolina allies thought they would easily be able to capture the main Spanish outpost in Florida. However, the Spanish had strengthened Fort San Marcos, and Oglethorpe and his followers were forced to begin a siege because they were unable to easily capture the fort. The siege was not very successful. The ships could not get close enough to the coast to attack the fort, and the land-based forces of Oglethorpe did not have any cannons big enough to do any damage to the fort's stone walls. Eventually, the colonists returned north, and Florida remained a Spanish colony until 1821, when it became part of the United States.

The final threat to the colony was the French. There were French colonies in Canada and Louisiana and the French hoped to connect the two by building outposts throughout the Mississippi River basin. This caused problems for all the English colonies that hoped to expand to the west or were close to Canada. South Carolina traders

Often referred to as the founder of Georgia, General James Oglethorpe was primarily concerned with the colony's defense, especially protecting the colony from the Spanish in Florida. *(Courtesy of Hargrett Rare Book & Manuscript Library/University of Georgia Libraries)*

found themselves competing with French traders at times. Between 1689 and 1763, four wars were fought between the English colonies and the French. These wars in North America coincided with larger wars fought in Europe.

The last of these wars is known as the French and Indian War or the Seven Years' War. It was fought from 1754 to 1763. Although the war was primarily fought to the north of South Carolina, hundreds of South Carolinians fought alongside the British troops. Thirteen years after the Seven Years' War, many of these same South Carolinians would be fighting against English troops in the War for Independence.

SOUTH CAROLINA BECOMES A ROYAL COLONY

From the standpoint of Cooper and the seven other original proprietors, Carolina had not turned out the way they had expected. The Fundamental Constitutions were never really implemented and their utopian colony was anything but that. The colonists who came to Carolina were an independent group who from the very beginning ignored the laws and rules of the proprietors and their agents. In addition to that, the quitrents, or rent, for the land that the proprietors were expecting to collect from the colonists never provided the anticipated profits. By the 1700s, some of the original proprietors had died, and those who had bought or inherited their shares were disenchanted with the problems that South Carolina presented.

For their part, the influential people in South Carolina often saw the proprietors as the enemy. They refused to cooperate with the governors the proprietors appointed and did everything possible to run the colony the way they wanted to. Other proprietary colonies had also failed to meet the expectations of investors. In addition, the Crown had decided it would be easier to manage the colonies if they were all uniformly organized. In the Northeast, many of the colonies had lost their original charters and become royal colonies. This created serious problems in some colonies. The colonists in South Carolina saw the idea of becoming a royal colony as a solution to their problems.

Between 1719 and 1729, there was near anarchy, or chaos, in the colony. The proprietors' governor, Robert Johnson, the son of one of the proprietors, refused to listen to the demands of people to be defended against a perceived Spanish threat. In the standoff that followed, 500 South Carolina militiamen took up arms. Johnson backed down and the colonists replaced him with James Moore, Jr.

With Moore as governor, the colony sent representatives to London to ask that South Carolina become a royal colony. Over the next 10 years, South Carolinians governed themselves as the proprietors negotiated with the Crown. Eventually, in 1729, seven of the eight proprietors agreed to sell their shares in Carolina back to the Crown for £17,500 plus back quitrents. John Carteret was the only holdout. He was finally given a large grant of land in North Carolina, known as the Granville Tract, in exchange for his share of South Carolina. In 1729, South Carolina became a royal colony.

SETTLING THE UP COUNTRY

All the early colonists in South Carolina settled along the coastal lowlands where they could grow rice and later indigo. Many of the planters became rich and had houses in Charleston where they lived during the social season. The plantations were limited to what South Carolinians came to call the "Low Country," a narrow strip of land along the coast and tidal rivers where rice could be grown along the edges of the swamps.

During his second term as governor, from 1730 to 1735, Robert Johnson proposed expanding the colony inland. His plan was known as "Johnson's township scheme." The plan called for the establishment of towns inland from the coast, in what South Carolinians refer to as the "Up Country." Colonists were recruited in England, Ireland, and Wales, as well as from other European countries such as Switzerland and the area that would become Germany. Over the next 30 years, as many as 8,000 people of German and Swiss-German heritage moved into the South Carolina Up Country. The towns of Amelia, Orangeburg, Florence, Williamsburg, Saxe-Gotha, and Society Hill were established at this time. Purrysburgh was also established at this time by Jean Pierre Purry.

Many of the Up Country settlers succeeded as small farmers and became an important part of colonial South Carolina. However, there were conflicts between the farmers of the Up Country and the wealthy planters of the Low Country. The Up Country

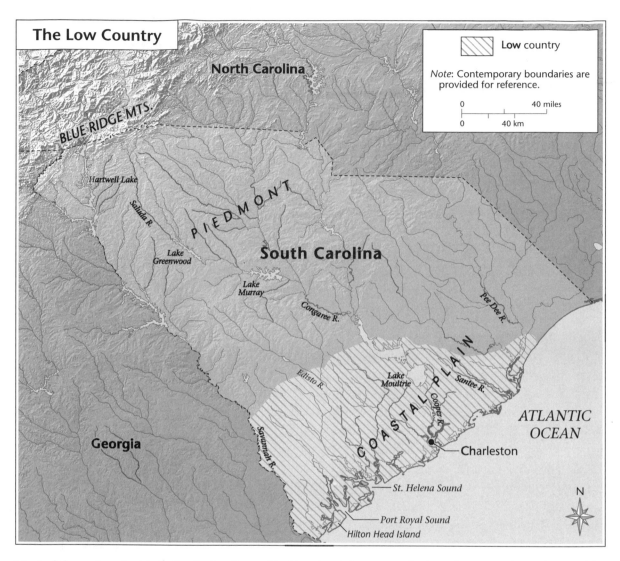

Most of the early colonists in South Carolina settled in what is known as the Low Country, where they could grow rice and other crops on large plantations worked by slaves.

farmers also had to deal with the Native Americans, whose lands they were settling on.

By 1730, intertribal warfare, conflicts with the colonists, raids by slave traders, and most important, disease had decimated the population of Native Americans in South Carolina. The last remaining stronghold for Native Americans was the homelands of the

Jean Pierre Purry

People came to the colonies with all sorts of grandiose plans. Jean Pierre Purry had one of the most interesting. Purry was Swiss and had come to the conclusion that the best climate in the world existed at 33° latitude. By the time he turned his attention to South Carolina, he had already been involved in two colonies that had failed at 33° south latitude, one in Australia and one in southern Africa.

Purry believed that a settlement at this latitude would also be ideal for growing the mulberry trees that were needed to raise silkworms and produce silk. His plan involved bringing 1,200 French Huguenots from Switzerland to South Carolina. The English Crown promised him 48,000 acres if he would bring at least 600 people and settle them in a place that would help defend the colony of South Carolina.

Purry agreed to the conditions, and in 1738 he arrived in the colony with between 600 and 700 people. They were sent up the Savannah River to the Great Yamasee Bluff. Instead of settling on the high ground of the bluff, Purrysburgh was built in the swampy land along the river. Malaria decimated the people, and by the early 1800s Purrysburgh disappeared from the map of South Carolina.

The French Huguenots from Switzerland Purry sent up the Savannah River decided to settle in swampy land bordering the river rather than on a bluff. The town they founded, Purrysburgh, was likely located on land similar to that in this photograph of the Savannah River near Savannah, Georgia. *(National Archives, Still Picture Records [NWDNS-165-SC-47])*

Cherokee in the Appalachian Mountains of Virginia and North and South Carolina. Up until 1758, the Cherokee had been staunch allies of the British in their wars against the French and their Native American allies. In 1758, a number of Cherokee helped the British achieve victory at the battle of Fort Duquesne, near present-day Pittsburgh, Pennsylvania.

On the way home from the battle, the militiamen from the Carolinas and Virginia argued with a group of Cherokee warriors. The disagreement escalated, and some people were killed on both sides. At this point, the Cherokee, who were feeling pressure on their mountain homelands by the encroachment of settlers, went to war against the colonists. The Cherokee raided along the frontier, and a force of white militia from South Carolina captured a few Cherokee. When it was learned that the Cherokee captives were murdered by the colonists, the warfare increased. The war lasted two years, until in 1761 the Cherokee signed a peace treaty in Charleston.

By the end of the Seven Years' War in 1763, South Carolina had grown to a colony of more than 94,000 people. Slaves still made up 60 percent of the colony. The Cherokee had been defeated. It seemed as though the future was secure. However, 12 years later the people of South Carolina would be some of the first to join the fight for independence for the thirteen English colonies in North America.

5

The Road to Revolution

After four wars in North America between the French and the British and their colonies, the Treaty of Paris in 1763 ended the French threat in North America. In Britain, government officials felt it was time for the colonies to pay their share of the costs of the wars. Previous attempts at regulating and taxing trade in the colonies had been poorly thought out and were mostly ignored by American merchants. There were also conflicts between the Crown and the elected state legislatures.

On December 22, 1771, yet another royal governor arrived in Charleston to try and control the uncooperative state legislators. Governor Thomas Boone wanted to show the wealthy planters who controlled the legislature that he was in charge. When Christopher Gadsden, who had been a vocal critic of previous royal governors and officials, was elected to the legislature in 1762, there had been some minor irregularities regarding the election officials. When Boone learned of this, he refused to allow Gadsden to take his seat in the legislature.

Instead of proving that he was in charge, Boone's actions instead created a controversy. The other members of the legislature pointed out that Gadsden was clearly the choice of the people in his district and should be allowed to take his seat. Boone quickly found out how powerful the legislators actually were. They voted to censure him, condemning his actions.

The debate was about the rights of the colonists to be governed by a legislature they elected. The governor believed the power

Christopher Gadsden
(1724–1805)

It took most of the people in South Carolina a long time to realize that independence was the only way they would get the rights they deserved. However, there were a few people who were calling for independence long before the delegates to the Second Continental Congress signed the Declaration of Independence. Christopher Gadsden was one of the first people in South Carolina to call for independence. In 1766, he wrote a newspaper article that declared in Latin, "Aut Mors, Aut Libertas," which translates as "either death or liberty."

Throughout the time before and during the Revolution, Gadsden was on the front lines. He was a member of the Sons of Liberty and often gave speeches at the Liberty Tree in Charleston. He commanded the First South Carolina Infantry at Fort Johnson in the first battle of Charleston in 1776. Gadsden also served as a delegate to both Continental Congresses where he helped start the Continental navy. He is given credit for the design of the navy's flag, which showed a coiled rattlesnake with the words "DON'T TREAD ON ME" beneath the snake.

When the British captured Charleston in 1780, Gadsden, who was lieutenant governor at the time, refused to leave the city with the other politicians. He vowed to give his life fighting the British. Although he did not die in the siege, he was captured and spent 10 months in solitary confinement in a prison in Florida. His health was so weakened when he came back to South Carolina that he declined to serve when elected governor after the War for Independence ended.

This flag is believed to be the first flag of the U.S. Marines and the Continental navy. The same coiled snake appeared on the drums of the early Marines. *(National Archives/DOD, War & Conflict, #26)*

rested with him as an appointee of the king. Boone ordered the local papers not to publish anything critical of him or his actions. Over the next two years, Boone tried to assert his authority. However, in 1764, Boone returned to England, where he resigned his position. The argument between the elected legislature and the royal governor would soon expand to the attempts by the British Parliament to tax the American colonies.

THE SUGAR ACT OF 1764

While Governor Boone struggled with the South Carolina legislature, the English Parliament passed its first attempt to tax the Americans. Sugar from the Caribbean was an important trade commodity, especially for the New England colonies that distilled molasses into rum. The rum was then traded on both sides of the Atlantic Ocean. The act passed by Parliament in 1764 tried to tax and regulate the trade in sugar and molasses. The people of South Carolina were never really concerned about the Sugar Act as it applied more to the northern colonies. The act exempted rice, which was the primary crop of the wealthy planters in South Carolina.

Even though the Sugar Act was never really effective, it caused concern. It showed that Parliament believed it could impose taxes on the people in the American colonies, even though they did not have any representatives in Parliament. When the Sugar Act was replaced by the Stamp Act in 1765, "no taxation without representation" became an issue throughout the thirteen colonies.

THE STAMP ACT OF 1765

Where the Sugar Act had applied to only a small segment of the business world in the colonies, the Stamp Act was planned to affect almost everybody. The Stamp Act required that all newspapers, legal documents, and some consumer goods such as playing cards have a tax stamp attached to them before they could be sold or filed. Long before the first stamp arrived, protestors throughout the colonies formed into semi-secret groups known as the Sons of Liberty. It would be these groups that would push the colonies toward independence and the war that was required to achieve it. In South Carolina, the Sons of Liberty took an active part in fighting the Stamp Act.

On October 18, 1765, the first shipment of stamps arrived in Charleston Harbor aboard the ship *Planters Adventure*. The ship was met by 2,000 protestors. They carried a gallows, used to hang criminals, with an effigy of the stamp distributor, and a coffin that was labeled "American Liberty." When the mob reached the end of Broad Street, they burned the effigy and buried the coffin.

The crowd went on to the houses of the men who were in charge of distributing the stamps and collecting the fees. Confronted by the large group, both men resigned their positions. The stamps were moved secretly to Fort Johnson and then put on the British warship HMS *Speedwell*. The protests had been successful. No stamps were issued in South Carolina.

However, the lack of stamps created a serious problem in Charleston. More than 100 ships were in port waiting to load the rice and indigo that had been harvested in 1765. Without stamps for their documents, the cargo could not be loaded on the ships. The more than 1,400 sailors wandering around the streets of Charleston posed a serious threat to the security of the people who lived there.

To avoid serious problems, a number of compromises were reached in South Carolina. Georgia, the colony to the south of South Carolina, was the only colony that ever issued any stamps. Some of the ships sent their paperwork to the port of Savannah,

Anno Regni

GEORGII III.

REGIS

Magnæ Britanniæ, Franciæ, & Hiberniæ,

QUINTO.

At the Parliament begun and holden at *Westminster*, the Nineteenth Day of *May, Anno. Dom.* 1761, in the First Year of the Reign of our Sovereign Lord *GEORGE* the Third, by the Grace of God, of *Great-Britain, France,* and *Ireland,* King, Defender of the Faith, *&c.*

And from thence continued by several Prorogations to the Tenth Day of *January,* 1765, being the Fourth Session of the Twelfth Parliament of *Great-Britain.*

LONDON:

Printed by *Mark Baskett,* Printer to the King's Most Excellent Majesty: And, re-printed by *James Parker,* in the Province of *New-Jersey.*

The beginning of the Stamp Act appears as printed in a 1766 manuscript in London. Its 1765 passage sparked protests by the colonists. *(Library of Congress)*

Georgia, to get the appropriate stamps so they could load up with goods and sail for England. Governor William Bull also helped avoid more serious problems by allowing some ships to leave without stamped documents. He created a special certificate that stated that the stamps were not available and allowed the ships to

Liberty Tree

Throughout the colonies, the Sons of Liberty designated meeting places. These were often outdoors under the spreading limbs of a tree. These trees became known as Liberty Trees. The one in Boston, Massachusetts, was a giant elm that was cut down by British soldiers during the Siege of Boston in 1775. It supposedly yielded 14 cords of firewood. The Liberty Tree in Charleston was an oak. When the city was captured by the British in 1780, they cut down the tree and then burned the stump.

The Patriots of Charleston dug up the roots of the Liberty Tree and made canes of them. Reportedly, Thomas Jefferson was presented with a cane from the roots of the Charleston Liberty Tree. The last remaining Liberty Tree from the time of the American Revolution was a huge poplar on the campus of St. John's College in Annapolis, Maryland. Over the years, people went to great lengths to keep the tree alive. It was finally cut down in 1999 after it was severely damaged by a hurricane.

William Bull governed South Carolina from 1764 to 1766. He lived in this house, built in the 18th century in Charleston and photographed in 1940. *(Library of Congress, Prints and Photographs Division [HABS, SC, 10-CHAR, 143-1])*

clear customs. Had the governor not done this, the fighting might have started even sooner in South Carolina.

Massachusetts called for the thirteen colonies to send representatives to a Stamp Act Congress in 1765 in New York to discuss a course of united action. Nine colonies, including South Carolina,

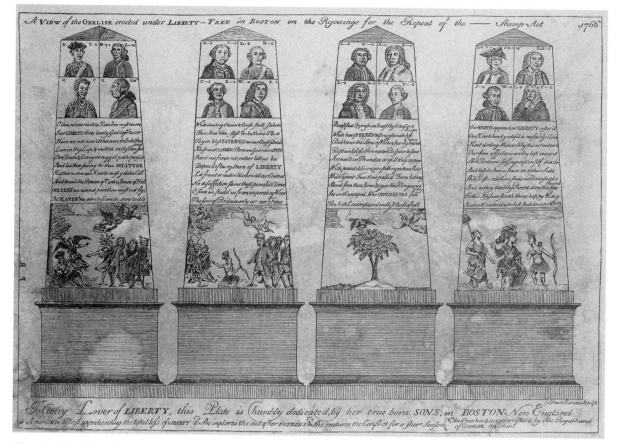

The obelisk whose four sides are shown here was created by Paul Revere and erected under the Liberty Tree on Boston Common in celebration of the Stamp Act's repeal. *(Library of Congress, Prints and Photographs Division [LC-USZC4-22385])*

sent delegates. Massachusetts, New York, New Jersey, Rhode Island, Pennsylvania, Delaware, Connecticut, and Maryland also sent representatives. The delegates from South Carolina were Christopher Gadsden, Thomas Lynch, and John Rutledge. Although the representatives at the congress considered themselves loyal subjects of the king, the resolutions they passed made it clear that they felt Parliament did not have the right to tax them.

Parliament realized that the Stamp Act would not work. They repealed it before it was ever really implemented. Rather than accept the total defeat of their attempt to tax the American colonies, Parliament passed the Declaratory Act in 1766. It stated that Parliament had the right to tax the colonies and pass whatever other laws they thought were needed to manage the British Empire. Parliament would not give up. The laws it passed that affected the colonies would push the colonists into the War for Independence.

THE TOWNSHEND DUTIES AND THE TEA AND INTOLERABLE ACTS

In 1767, Parliament tried again to raise tax revenue in the American colonies. This time they passed a series of taxes, called the Townshend Duties, on certain goods that were imported into the colonies from England and other parts of the British Empire. The duties were on glass, red and white lead, paints, paper, and tea. The money that came from these duties was to be used to pay the salaries of Crown officials in America. At the same time, Parliament also gave more authority to its customs service in America.

The reaction to the Townshend Duties was again widespread. The people of Boston, Massachusetts, one of the more radical communities in the colonies, decided to protest the duties by not importing any of the goods listed in the law. This idea quickly spread throughout the colonies.

In South Carolina, Gadsden and others wrote articles, which were published in the newspapers, calling for the people of the colony to join the boycott of British goods. The wealthy planters of South Carolina were relatively self-sufficient on their plantations, and the boycott caused them little inconvenience. The artisans and

The Seizing of the Sloop *Active*
(1767)

In May 1767, James Hawker, the commander of the British ship *Sadoine*, seized the sloop *Active*, which was a Charleston-based merchant ship. The ship was suspected of trying to bring goods into the port illegally. The seizure of the *Active* upset many of the merchants in Charleston. This event convinced many of the city's merchants that it was time to join the Patriot cause.

craftsmen joined the boycott willingly as they often had to compete against imported goods. The merchants who sold imported goods, however, were the ones who were hurt the most by the boycott. Naturally, they were reluctant to join in.

On July 22, 1769, a large meeting took place in Charleston under the Liberty Tree. People from all the different interest groups met and came up with an agreement for the boycott of British goods. A committee was established with 13 members from each of the three main groups in Charleston—planters, artisans, and merchants. Soon all but a handful of people had agreed to the boycott.

Like the Sugar Act and the Stamp Act before it, the Townshend Duties failed to raise the money Parliament expected. Instead, they increased the feelings of hostility between the colonies and the Crown. In 1770, the Townshend Duties, except the tax on tea, were all repealed. The duty on tea remained for a number of reasons.

Parliament did not want to give in completely to the colonists. Also, through the East India Company, there was a monopoly on tea imported into the colonies. Despite the fact that most of the duties had been lifted, the colonists continued their boycott of tea.

In 1773, Parliament tried another approach with the Tea Act. This time, they lowered the price of tea. British tea was still taxed, but it was cheaper than non-British tea that was smuggled into the colonies. Parliament believed that the Americans would put their wallets ahead of their principles.

Parliament was wrong. The principle of "no taxation without representation" was more important than saving a little money. When the first shipment of tea under the new Tea Act arrived in Boston, Massachusetts, it was promptly dumped into the harbor by the Sons of Liberty who disguised themselves as Native Americans. The "Boston Tea Party" on December 16, 1773, brought the situation between the British and their American colonies to the boiling point.

The Boston Tea Party is the best known but not the only "tea party." The Sons of Liberty in many of the colonies followed the example of those in Boston. The Charleston Tea Party took place on November 1, 1774, when a shipment of British tea was dumped into the harbor.

This lithograph shows male colonists dumping hundreds of cases of tea into the harbor in December 1773 in an event that became known as the Boston Tea Party. Charleston followed Boston's example with its own "tea party" 11 months later. *(National Archives/DOD, War & Conflict, #3)*

Parliament's reaction to the Boston Tea Party was extremely harsh and led to the first armed conflicts between the colonies and Britain. Parliament passed what they called the Coercive Acts, but in the colonies, it was known as the Intolerable Acts. Part of the acts was known as the Boston Port Bill, and it instructed the British navy to close the port of Boston. No ships were to be let in or out of Boston until the tea that had been dumped into the harbor was paid for.

Parliament was planning to teach the colonies a lesson. However, rather than give into these harsh measures, the colonies rallied together to help the residents of Boston. The people of South Carolina sent large quantities of rice to other ports in Massachusetts. The rice was then delivered to Boston over land. As a result

Chosen at a meeting in Charleston to represent South Carolina, Henry Middleton participated in the first Continental Congress. *(Library of Congress, Prints and Photographs Division [LC-USZ6-833])*

of the Intolerable Acts, the patriot leaders of the colonies called for another gathering of representatives from all thirteen colonies.

THE FIRST CONTINENTAL CONGRESS

The Stamp Act Congress of 1765 set the stage for the First Continental Congress. One united voice from the colonies seemed to be more effective than 13 separate ones. When the call went out in June 1774, through the Committees of Correspondence, for a meeting of delegates from all thirteen colonies, the people of South Carolina were quick to respond.

By this time, there were really two governments in South Carolina. The royal governor and his council tried to implement the laws of Parliament and the instructions they received from the Crown. At the same time, a steering committee had been created in Charleston by those opposed to the actions of Parliament and the Crown. This committee called for a general meeting in July 1774 to discuss a plan of action and to elect representatives to the Continental Congress.

Almost every community in the colony sent delegates to the meeting in Charleston, and they elected Christopher Gadsden, Thomas Lynch, Henry Middleton, and the brothers John and Edward Rutledge to represent South Carolina. The delegates were given the authority to pledge South Carolina's support to whatever the Congress decided.

Committees of Correspondence

In the 18th century, it was difficult to communicate ideas and information over long distances. There were very few newspapers in the colonies and none of the electronic media we depend on today existed. The Boston, Massachusetts, town meeting decided in 1772 to set up a committee that would "state the Rights of the Colonists" and share them with other communities in Massachusetts. The Committee of Correspondence worked so well that the idea soon spread to all the colonies. It was through the Committees of Correspondence that the call for the First Continental Congress went out.

When they convened in Philadelphia in September 1774, only the most radical among the delegates to the First Continental Congress were thinking about independence. Three of the most vocal were Samuel Adams of Massachusetts, Patrick Henry of Virginia, and Christopher Gadsden of South Carolina. The more moderate voices at the First Continental Congress prevailed, and reconciliation was still foremost in people's minds.

The First Continental Congress called for a general boycott of goods from the British Empire and made plans to have a Second Continental Congress on May 10, 1775. The Second Congress was to assess the situation after the Crown had a chance to respond and do whatever was needed at that time. It is unlikely that anyone attending the First Continental Congress would have predicted that by the meeting of the Second Continental Congress, fighting would have begun between Britain and the colonies and that their next resolution would be the Declaration of Independence.

THE END OF ROYAL GOVERNMENT

Shortly after word arrived from the First Continental Congress, Patriots in South Carolina set up a provincial congress to run the colony and prepare for the possibility of armed conflict with the British. Governor Lord William Campbell arrived in the colony in June 1775. He lasted only a few months and was the last royal governor of South Carolina.

Governor Campbell had arrived amid rumors he had brought arms for the Loyalists and was also planning to incite the slaves and Native Americans in South Carolina to rebel. The rumors were false. However, the people of the Low Country were so concerned, they spied on the governor and learned he was plotting with Loyalists in the backcountry.

On September 15, 1775, fearing for his safety as a mob approached his house, Governor Campbell snuck aboard a British ship in Charleston Harbor. When the ship sailed for England, the governor went with it, and the South Carolinians were free to govern themselves.

The provincial congress was quick to organize a new government, and in spring 1776, they appointed Christopher Gadsden, John Rutledge, Henry Laurens, and others to draft a constitution. There were a number of interesting points in South Carolina's first constitution. Although 60 percent of the voters lived away from the coast, they were given only one-third of the seats in the legislature. The constitution created a legislative council. The president of the council, John Rutledge, also served as chief executive of South Carolina.

It is important to note that under British law at the time, the president of the council served as the acting governor in the absence of the governor. It appeared at this point that the South Carolinians were still leaving the door open for the return of British rule. South Carolina was only the second state, New Hampshire being the first, to adopt a new constitution.

6

The War for Independence Begins

On April 19, 1775, the first battle between colonial militia and British troops took place at Lexington and Concord, Massachusetts. Before this, many in the colonies had begun to prepare for the possibility of armed conflict. In South Carolina, a provincial congress had been established that was the government for those in the colony who were sympathetic to the Patriot cause. At the same time, many people in South Carolina, especially the small farmers of the backcountry, remained loyal to the Crown and were known as Loyalists.

There are many theories surrounding the reasons why people remained Loyalists during the American Revolution. In South Carolina, those in the Up Country had more differences with the wealthy planters of the Low Country than they did with the Crown. Others have suggested that because many of the backcountry settlers were of German descent, as was George III, king of England, they remained loyal to the Crown. For whatever reason, the first bloodshed in South Carolina was not between British troops and Americans. It was between Loyalists and Patriots.

REGULATORS, LOYALISTS, AND PATRIOTS

In the 20 years before the War for Independence, many people moved into the Up Country of South Carolina. At first, there were no courts, jails, or law enforcement people. Throughout the history of the United States, the frontier was often a place of lawlessness. This was as true when the frontier was east of the Appalachian Mountains as it was later when Americans settled the vast western regions of the country.

In South Carolina and other colonies, groups of settlers organized to protect themselves from attack by outlaws and the Native Americans whose lands they were encroaching on. As time went on, the Regulators, as they became known as in South Carolina, became better organized. They used their influence to seek more equitable government from the wealthy planters who controlled the government in Charleston. The Regulators developed into a well-trained militia, and many of them fought in the Revolution, some as Patriots and some as Loyalists.

During the American Revolution, more than 130 battles were fought in South Carolina, a greater number than in any other colony. The first was November 19–21, 1775, at the frontier settlement of Ninety Six. There were no British troops involved. Instead, 600 Patriots attacked the fort where more than 1,200 Loyalists were encamped. The fighting was relatively light, and only one Patriot and a few Loyalists were killed. Later in the war, the British expanded the fort at Ninety Six, and a major battle took place there.

Although only a few people died at Ninety Six, the battle set the stage for a long and bitter fight between the two groups in South Carolina. Throughout the war, both Loyalists and Patriots treated each other harshly. At first, the Patriots had the upper hand. However, when the British captured Charleston in 1780, the Loyalists rallied to their cause.

THE FIRST BATTLE OF CHARLESTON

In spring 1776, the government in Charleston heard that the British were planning to attack and capture the port. South Carolinians prepared for the British. Four thousand troops flooded into Charleston to defend the city. Most of them were from South Carolina, but small numbers of troops arrived from North Carolina and Virginia. On Sullivans Island outside Charleston, under the leadership of Colonel William Moultrie, a fort was hastily built using palmetto logs from local palm trees.

Major General Charles Lee, a former professional British soldier who had joined the Patriot cause and was the third highest

Photographed in 1865 and located on Sullivans Island, Fort Moultrie was used to defend South Carolina in both the Revolutionary War and and the Civil War. *(Library of Congress, Prints and Photographs Division [LC-B8171-3067])*

ranking officer in the Continental army, arrived with the Virginia and North Carolina troops. His arrival gave the South Carolinians a much needed morale boost. However, Lee was not very impressed with the preparations for the defense of the city. He thought the fort on Sullivans Island, which was soon called Fort Moultrie, would be a "slaughter pen."

Fort Johnson on James Island was more substantial, but it was not in very good condition. The Patriot forces waited in the two forts and in batteries in Charleston while on June 28, 1776, two British 50-gun ships, five frigates, and a bomb vessel, a small ship that carried mortars for bombing land-based targets, sailed into

The Palmetto State

South Carolina is unofficially known as the "Palmetto State." The palmetto is a type of palm tree that grows up to 36 feet in height and can be found along the North American coast from Florida to North Carolina. After the battle of Fort Moultrie, the likeness of a palmetto tree was added to the flag of South Carolina. It later became the state tree. It is impossible to know what would have happened had not the soft palmetto logs absorbed the cannon fire from the British ships, but it is safe to assume that the outcome of the battle would have been different.

The original name of South Carolina, *Chicora,* appears at the top of this illustrated sheet-music cover printed in 1861, but the focus of the image is a scene that includes a palmetto tree, the unofficial symbol of South Carolina. *(Library of Congress, Prints and Photographs Division [LC-USZ62-91834])*

Charleston harbor. The British had put army forces ashore on one of the outer islands and assumed they would be able to wade across to the mainland. The water was too deep and the current too strong, so the navy had to attack without the aid of ground forces.

At first appearance, Fort Moultrie looked like it would fold after the first broadside. However, the spongy palmetto logs absorbed shot after shot. After the first night of bombardment, Moultrie and his men were still in position, and approximately 40 men had been injured. Three of the British frigates ran aground. One, the *Actaeon,* was destroyed by its captain and crew rather than allow the rebels to capture it.

The British force realized it would take more to capture Charleston than they had planned for. A number of the ships in the fleet had sustained damage from the two forts and shore batteries. The British decided to cut their losses, collect their stranded soldiers, and leave Charleston to the colonials. Neither side probably thought it would be four years before the British forces once again turned their attention to Charleston.

DECLARING INDEPENDENCE

At the end of the First Continental Congress, the delegates voted to convene a second congress the following year to reassess the boycott they had called for in the First Continental Congress. Before the Second Continental Congress met in Philadelphia in 1775, fighting had broken out in South Carolina. Then the British attacked Charleston in 1776. Despite this, there were still a lot of people in South Carolina who were reluctant to break away from the Crown.

Life was good for many people in South Carolina in the 18th century. Independence from Britain would mean an uncertain future. When it was time to vote for the Declaration of Independence at the Second Continental Congress, the South Carolina Delegation consisted of Arthur Middleton; Thomas Lynch, Jr.; Thomas Heyward, Jr.; and Edward Rutledge.

When the state delegations to the Second Continental Congress were polled on July 1, 1776, it looked like only nine states were ready to vote in favor of the Declaration of Independence. Only two delegates from Delaware were present, and one voted for and one against. The delegates from New York had been instructed not

During the Second Continental Congress, Thomas Lynch, Jr., voted against the Declaration of Independence in a trial poll, along with the other three delegates from South Carolina and the Pennsylvania delegates. *(Library of Congress, Prints and Photographs Division [LC-USZ61-461])*

to vote. The delegates from Pennsylvania and South Carolina voted against the Declaration. Without all thirteen colonies, there would be real problems for everyone.

Late on July 2, another trial vote was taken. Caesar Rodney, the third delegate from Delaware, had ridden through a stormy night to break the tie in the state's delegation by voting for the Declaration. Pennsylvania persuaded two delegates who were opposed to independence to abstain. New York still did not vote, but let it be known that they would most likely agree. Edward Rutledge, who at 26 years old was the youngest delegate at the Congress, said that South Carolina would not be the only state to vote against independence when the final vote was taken.

On July 4, 1776, all thirteen colonies voted in favor of the Declaration of Independence. There would be no turning back from a war with Britain. When the official signing took place, all four of the delegates from South Carolina put their signatures at the bottom of the document. On August 5,

The First Paragraph of the Declaration of Independence

When in the Course of human events, it becomes necessary for one people to dissolve the political bands which have connected them with another, and to assume among the Powers of the earth, the separate and equal station to which the Laws of Nature and of Nature's God entitle them, a decent respect to the opinions of mankind requires that they should declare the causes which impel them to the separation.

Thomas Heyward, Jr., served as a South Carolina delegate to the Second Continental Congress and fought in the Revolutionary War. A house he built in Charleston around 1750, shown in this photograph, is now a museum. *(Library of Congress, Prints and Photographs Division [HABS, SC, 10-CHAR, 103-9])*

1776, the Declaration of Independence was read aloud in Charleston. The members of the provincial assembly and the state militia held a parade and fired off cannons. When the Declaration of Independence was read, people cheered.

7

The War for Independence Comes to South Carolina

THE BRITISH TAKE OVER SOUTH CAROLINA

At first, the War for Independence was fought in the North, with the British hanging on to New York and capturing Philadelphia. General George Washington spent hard winters in New Jersey and at Valley Forge, Pennsylvania. In South Carolina in 1776, the Cherokee joined the British side and began attacking frontier settlements. South Carolina responded by sending out a force of 4,000 militia, who destroyed many villages and killed more than 2,000 Cherokee.

In 1777, the Cherokee gave up their claim to the land that would become South Carolina's four westernmost counties. With the Cherokee threat neutralized, the only fighting that took place in South Carolina was sporadic clashes between Loyalist and Patriot South Carolinians. Many South Carolinians went north and fought with the Continental army against the British. The relative peace in South Carolina came to an end in 1780.

In 1778, with the war in the North at a stalemate, Britain decided to turn its attention to the South. The British believed there were still many Loyalists in Georgia and South Carolina. The thinking was that if the British could take over the Patriot governments, then the Loyalists would declare their support for the Crown and help the British troops.

The British started in Georgia. They captured Savannah in December 1778. During 1779, they captured much of the rest of Georgia and then turned their attention to South Carolina. Unlike the first attack on Charleston, the British arrived in February 1780, with a huge fleet and 10,000 soldiers.

Sir Henry Clinton, the British commander, had planned for an extended siege. After months of pounding from the artillery on

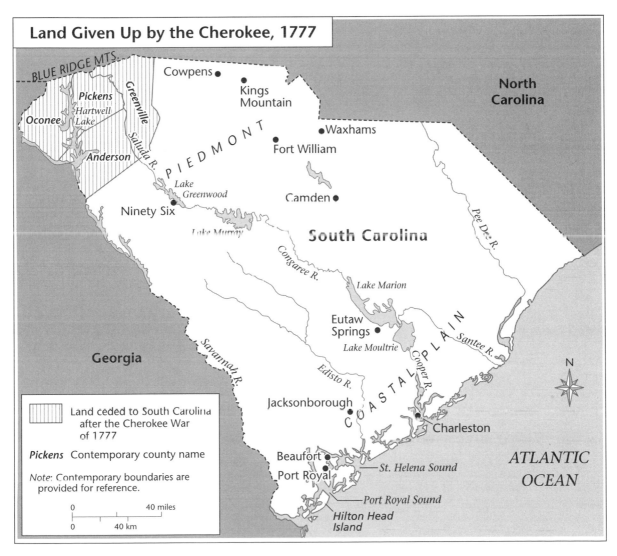

Land Given Up by the Cherokee, 1777

Land ceded to South Carolina after the Cherokee War of 1777

Pickens Contemporary county name

Note: Contemporary boundaries are provided for reference.

0 — 40 miles
0 — 40 km

After the Cherokee War of 1777, the Cherokee were forced to give up land in western South Carolina. That land became the four westernmost counties of the state.

Midway through the Revolutionary War, Sir Henry Clinton (above) was appointed commander in chief of the British forces when General William Howe resigned. This engraving was published between 1770 and 1780. *(Library of Congress, Prints and Photographs Division [LC-USZ62-45188])*

land and the ships in the harbor, Charleston fell to the British on May 12, 1780. The fall of Charleston was the worst defeat suffered by the Americans during the Revolutionary War.

The British captured 5,000 men, 400 cannons, 6,000 muskets, and a large supply of American gunpowder. With the majority of the American army in the South captured, the British quickly seized the rest of the state. They established outposts throughout the backcountry, as well as holding Charleston and the Low Country.

As hoped, the Loyalists were quick to rally behind the British. In 1780 and 1781, there were many battles between Loyalists and Patriots. It has been reported that the Loyalists were so brutal in their attacks on the Patriots that even the British soldiers were startled. It was at this time that some of South Carolina's most famous Patriots gained notoriety.

With the British in control of the state, many of the Patriots gathered under a few of their leaders and fought a guerrilla campaign against the British and their Loyalist allies. Francis Marion, who was called "the Swamp Fox," hid out with his troop in the swamps of the Low Country and raided British targets and Loyalist plantations. Thomas Sumter led a similar group in the middle part of the state. Sumter was known as "the Gamecock." A gamecock was a rooster that was raised for fighting other roosters. Cockfighting was popular and considered a sport at the time. The third guerrilla leader was Andrew Pickens. He and his troop fought in the western part of the state.

With the guerrilla warfare of Marion, Sumter, and Pickens on one side and brutal attacks by British and Loyalist forces on the other, no part of South Carolina was left untouched. Fields, settlements, and plantations throughout the state were destroyed.

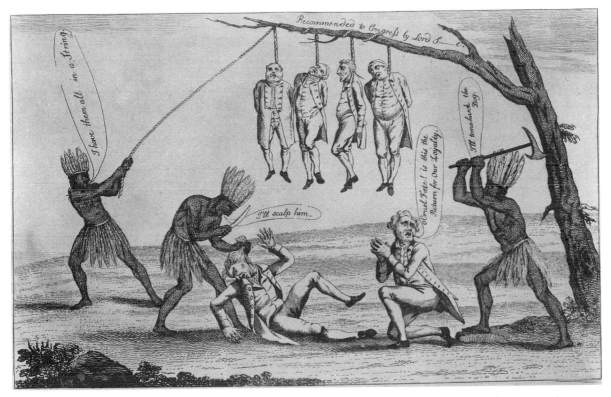

American Indians fought on both sides of the Revolutionary War, but in this British political cartoon, three American Indians murder six Loyalists—four are dead and hanging from a tree and two more will soon share their fate. *(Library of Congress, Prints and Photographs Division [LC-USZ62-1540])*

Guerrilla Warfare

The word *guerrilla* is Spanish and literally means "little war." It was first used in the 19th century when the Spanish were trying to repel a French invasion. However, the tactics of guerrilla warfare had been around since people started fighting wars. In guerrilla warfare, a small group of fighters, who are usually from the area, attack the supplies and military outposts of a larger, often invading army. The attacks are brief and intended to harass the enemy. After the attack, the guerrilla fighters quickly retreat to a place where it is difficult for the enemy to find them.

The Swamp Fox
(1732–1795)

Francis Marion was one of the best known heroes of the American Revolution in South Carolina. He first served in the South Carolina militia during the Seven Years' War, during which he fought in the battle between the South Carolina troops and the Cherokee in 1761. In this battle, he and 30 men led the attack on the Cherokee, and 21 of his men died around him before the main colonial force entered the battle and defeated the Cherokee.

When Charleston fell to the British in 1780, Marion would have been captured with the more than 5,000 colonial soldiers had he not injured his ankle and gone home to heal. Before the battle, a group of officers had locked themselves in a house in Charleston so no one would disturb their party. Marion was from a French Huguenot family and did not drink alcohol. Rather than take part in the party, he jumped out a second story window and broke his ankle.

As a result of the incident, Marion would have a limp for the rest of his life, but fortunately for South Carolina and the Patriot cause, it did not slow him down. As the leader of a band of about 100 guerrilla fighters, he harassed the British forces in South Carolina. His tactics of sneaking out of the swamps at night, attacking quickly, and then disappearing back into the swamps before the British could organize a response made his force extremely effective. Colonel Banastre Tarleton, an officer who led a force of Loyalists, is credited with saying, "As for this damned swamp fox, the Devil himself could not catch him."

Marion's nickname stuck, and he has continued to be a popular character from the time period. From 1959 to 1961, ABC television aired a show entitled *The Swamp Fox,* based on Francis Marion's exploits during the Revolution. More recently, Mel Gibson's character in the movie, *The Patriot* (2000), was in part based on Marion.

Atrocities were committed by both sides. Within a short period of time after the fall of Charleston, the entire state of South Carolina was a very dangerous place to live.

THE BATTLE OF CAMDEN

After the fall of Charleston, some of the Continental forces that were able to escape headed for North Carolina. Clinton, the British commander in South Carolina, sent General Lord Cornwallis with

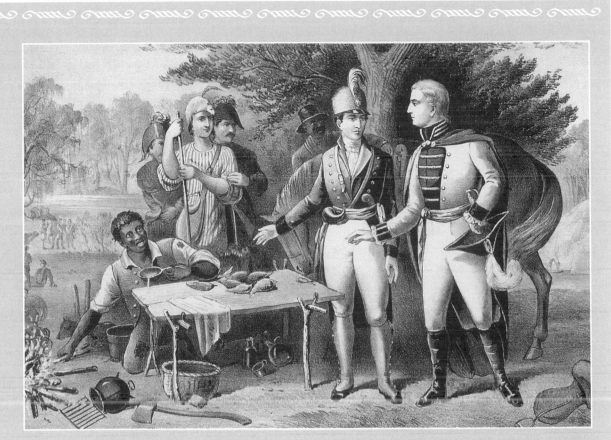

Francis Marion's guerrilla fighting methods in the South Carolina swamps during the Revolutionary War earned him the nickname "the Swamp Fox." *(Library of Congress, Prints and Photographs Division [LC-USZC2-2405])*

a force of 2,500 men to capture the remnants of the forces that had defended Charleston. The British forces were unable to catch up with the 350 fleeing Continental soldiers under the command of Colonel Abraham Buford.

Cornwallis sent Colonel Banastre Tarleton with 270 Loyalist cavalry ahead to catch Buford. On May 29, 1780, they caught up with and surprised the Patriot force at Waxhams, close to the North Carolina border. Tarleton's troops attacked suddenly and brutally. Using swords and bayonets, Tarleton's men quickly killed 113, while the Loyalists only lost 19. The Loyalists also captured 203 prisoners. Buford escaped to report the battle for which the Loyalist leader earned the nickname Bloody Tarleton.

The Continental Congress had appointed General Horatio Gates commander of the Southern Department of the Continental army. Hearing of the losses in South Carolina, General Gates headed south with a poorly trained and meagerly supplied force of 2,100 soldiers. Gates was soon joined by 2,000 North Carolina militiamen. The British forces under Cornwallis waited for Gates at Camden. On August 16, 1780, the two forces met in a pitched battle.

The American forces included many new recruits who were poorly trained and had never faced the British in a traditional European-style battle where both sides line up and fight until someone quits. The American troops were also weakened by the march south. Many of the men were sick, and only about 3,000 of them were able to take the field against the British regulars. Gates, who had been in the British army, arranged his forces in traditional European style and withdrew well behind the lines.

When Cornwallis gave the order to advance against Gates's right flank, the untrained Americans soon broke and fled. When the retreating soldiers came past his command post, Gates thought the battle was already lost. He mounted a fast horse and fled to North Carolina. The more seasoned American forces held for a while on the left flank but they were soon overwhelmed by the now numerically superior British. Those who retreated were pursued by Bloody Tarleton and his Loyalist cavalry.

When the final tally was made, more than 900 Americans had been killed and

Appointed by the Continental Congress, General Horatio Gates led the Southern Department of the Continental army briefly—until the American forces experienced a terrible defeat at the Battle of Camden and Nathanael Greene replaced him. *(Library of Congress, Prints and Photographs Division [LC-USZ62-45258])*

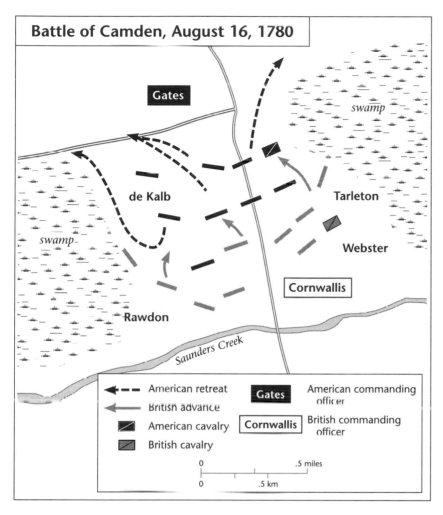

Battle of Camden, August 16, 1780

Gates

swamp

de Kalb

Tarleton

Webster

swamp

Cornwallis

Rawdon

Saunders Creek

- - ◄ American retreat	**Gates**	American commanding officer
← British advance	Cornwallis	British commanding officer
◼ American cavalry		
◼ British cavalry		

0 — .5 miles
0 — .5 km

General Horatio Gates made an ill-advised forced march to attack British supplies at Camden. He lost more than one-third of his force in the battle and left before the battle was over.

1,000 had been captured. Of the 4,100 Americans who had marched to Camden, only 700 reached the safety of North Carolina in the three days following the battle. Gates's actions were excused by a military tribunal. However, after the defeat of Camden, he retired to his plantation in Virginia and never commanded again.

The situation looked dire for the Patriot cause in South Carolina after the Battle of Camden. Cornwallis and his Loyalist sympathizers seemed to be firmly in command of the state. However, the actions of Marion and the other guerrilla leaders caused numerous problems. Then, in October 1780, the tide turned as the Patriots won a significant battle at Kings Mountain.

THE BATTLE OF KINGS MOUNTAIN

General Lord Cornwallis had plans to solidify his position in South Carolina, take North Carolina, and then move into Virginia, which he considered the center of the American rebellion. He recruited and trained Loyalists to hunt down Patriot forces in the Up Country. One such force of about 1,000 Loyalists was put under the command of Major Patrick Ferguson.

After some initial success in his mission to control the left flank of the main army, Ferguson proclaimed that he would destroy the countryside if the remaining Patriots did not surrender to him. His belligerent attitude backfired, and every able-bodied man on the frontier with a hunting rifle joined with others from Georgia, North Carolina, and Virginia to fight Ferguson and his Loyalists. There was no one commander of the Patriot force.

When Ferguson learned that a Patriot force was coming after him, he made a tactical mistake. He was only 35 miles from the main army but chose instead to stand and fight. The place he picked was the top of a ridge at Kings Mountain, South Carolina. Although he had the high ground, he neglected to fortify the position and soon learned that a force of backwoodsmen clad in buckskin hunting clothes was a formidable opponent.

Civil War

The battle of Kings Mountain points out an important fact. Although it was the thirteen colonies fighting for independence from the British, there were many in the colonies who did not want to break away from Britain. They considered themselves loyal British citizens. At Kings Mountain, Major Patrick Ferguson was the only person in the battle who was not an American. Without their Loyalist supporters, the British would not have been able to hang on in the war as long as they did. At the end of the war, many Loyalists were forced to leave the colonies, others left by choice.

On October 7, 1780, the Patriots came upon Ferguson's position and surrounded it. They were able to take cover in the woods on the slopes of the ridge where they could fire with great accuracy.

When Ferguson realized his force would eventually be wiped out by the Patriot snipers, he ordered a bayonet charge. The American rifles were not equipped with bayonets, so instead of meeting the charge, they fell back and continued to shoot. Twice Loyalists tried to raise a white flag to surrender, only to have it cut down by their commander. In a final move of desperation, Ferguson led a mounted charge down the hill. He was shot six times before he fell from his horse and died. All those who charged down the hill with

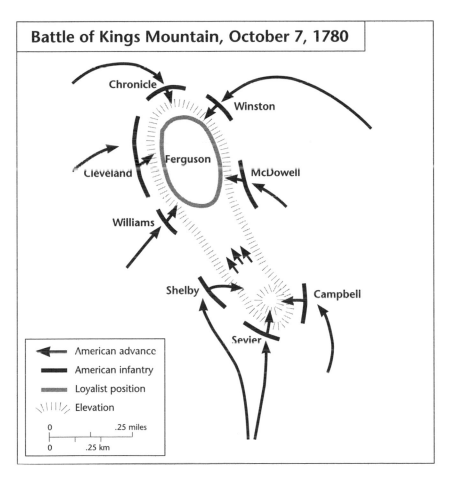

The defeat of the British at Kings Mountain, South Carolina, forced General Cornwallis to change his plan of marching north to Virginia.

Rifles versus Muskets

The Loyalists were equipped with British muskets that were designed for the close fighting of traditional European warfare. The smoothbore of the musket reduced the accuracy of the weapon to less than 90 yards. They were heavy and could have a bayonet, a sharp spearlike blade, attached to the front. Soldiers were trained to use their muskets in hand-to-hand combat, where they would use it to stab and club their enemies.

The hunting rifles of the Patriots had grooves in the barrel that were designed to spin the fired ball. The spin gave the ball greater stability as it traveled through the air and an effective range more than three times that of a musket. The American rifles were much lighter and not designed for close fighting.

him died as well. With Ferguson dead, those remaining on the top of the ridge surrendered.

However, the Patriots wanted revenge for the brutal treatment "Bloody Tarleton" had given Buford's men. The fighting continued for a few minutes after the white flag went up, and even more Loyalists were killed. In the end, the toll on the Loyalist force was 700 captured, 163 wounded, and 157 killed. The Patriot force sustained 28 killed and a little more than twice that number wounded.

The defeat of Major Ferguson forced Cornwallis to change his plans. Instead of continuing north into North Carolina, he retreated to near Winnsboro, South Carolina. He decided to spend the winter there and regroup for a spring offensive. The Americans, however, were not interested in waiting until spring. General Nathanael Greene was selected to replace Gates, and he decided to continue to press Cornwallis in South Carolina.

THE BATTLE OF COWPENS

General Greene split his force and sent General Daniel Morgan with a mixed force of 1,000 into western South Carolina. While the main army under General Greene harassed Cornwallis, Morgan's force captured Fort William, South Carolina, which had been held by a Loyalist force. Fearing that Morgan would work his way around and attack the main army from the rear, Cornwallis sent Colonel Tarleton with 1,100 men to deal with Morgan.

When Morgan heard that Tarleton was after him, he moved his force to a place known as the Cowpens. This was a large clearing in northwestern South Carolina where people along the frontier would bring their cattle to sell. By the time Morgan arrived at the Cowpens and prepared for battle, he had 600 Continental soldiers, most of whom were from Delaware and Maryland. These were

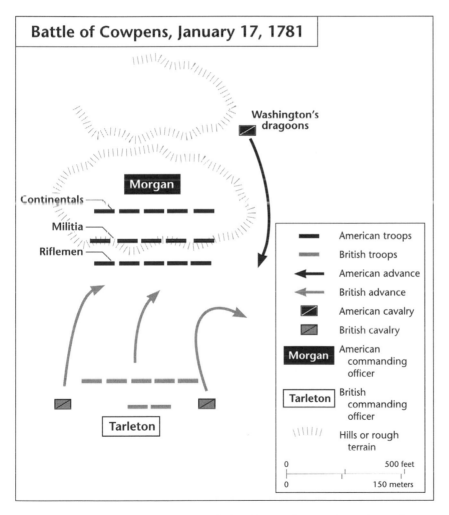

Battle of Cowpens, January 17, 1781

Washington's dragoons

Morgan

Continentals

Militia

Riflemen

Tarleton

	American troops
	British troops
←	American advance
←	British advance
	American cavalry
	British cavalry
Morgan	American commanding officer
Tarleton	British commanding officer
|||||	Hills or rough terrain

0   500 feet

0   150 meters

The defeat of the British at Cowpens helped bring the War for Independence to an end in South Carolina.

experienced soldiers who had fought at Camden and elsewhere. He also had 200 riflemen from Virginia, 500 militiamen from Georgia and the Carolinas, and a small contingent of mounted dragoons under the command of Lieutenant Colonel William Washington.

As Morgan prepared to fight the British force on January 17, 1781, he knew that the unseasoned militiamen would not stand for a steady assault from the British force, so he instructed them to take the front line, fire their first volley, and then retreat. He did the same with his second line as well. Not realizing that the retreat was part of the plan, Tarleton's troops rushed forward only to find the seasoned Continentals waiting for them. The sustained and accurate fire from the Continentals had a devastating affect on the British. To finish off the British force, Morgan had held Washington's mounted soldiers in reserve, hidden in the woods. As Tarleton realized he had been lured in, the Patriot cavalry charged out of the woods and cut off any escape route for most of his men.

Tarleton and Washington fought each other on the battlefield, but Tarleton realized the day was lost and was able to escape. Almost 350 members of the British force were killed or wounded, and 600 were captured. The Battle of Cowpens showed that the American military leaders had learned how to use their resources to get the advantage. The British had lost the initiative in South Carolina and would continue to give ground throughout 1781.

THE WAR COMES TO AN END

The American forces continued to fight their way through North and South Carolina. They captured many small garrisons and fought at least two major battles. The first was against Cornwallis at Guilford Courthouse near Greensboro, North Carolina, on March 15, 1781. Although Cornwallis could claim Guilford Courthouse as a victory, it was a hollow one. More than a quarter of his force was killed or wounded, and he had to continue his retreat.

By September, Cornwallis had gone to oversee the war in Virginia, and Lord Rawdon who had replaced him in South Carolina had left for England. It fell to Lieutenant Colonel Alexander Stewart to try and hold on to South Carolina for the British. General Greene caught up with the retreating British at Eutaw Springs on September 8, 1781, where another major battle was fought. Although the British could claim to have held off the Americans, they again sustained devastating losses. Stewart was forced to retreat to the last stronghold of the British at Charleston. The final battle of the war took place at Yorktown, Virginia, from September 28 to October 18, 1781. With the surrender of Cornwallis at Yorktown, the war was over. The 13 united states had won their independence and in many places, like South Carolina, would need to rebuild what the long war had destroyed.

8

The Struggle to Rebuild South Carolina

The American Revolution brought more destruction to South Carolina than to any of the 12 other colonies. Officially, 137 battles and skirmishes were fought within South Carolina's borders. In addition, raids by Loyalists against Patriots and Patriots against Loyalists disrupted the state even more. By the time the British evacuated Charleston on December 13, 1782, conditions in the state were disheartening.

Fields were untended, livestock had wandered off, and between 25,000 and 30,000 slaves had either escaped or been removed by the British. The government and people of South Carolina were deeply in debt as a result of the war. They also had to deal with those Loyalists who had chosen to stay in South Carolina. In 1782, the assembly elected Christopher Gadsden South Carolina's first governor after the war. Gadsden was in ill health and declined the office. It then fell to John Mathews to lead the state.

ADJUSTING TO INDEPENDENCE

Among the many battles and raids that took place in South Carolina, the majority pitted American Loyalists against American Patriots. Neighbors fought neighbors, and in some cases members of the same family were on opposing sides. When the war ended, dealing with the remaining Loyalists created serious problems.

Even before the British were out of Charleston early in 1782, a new state assembly met in Jacksonborough, about 30 miles from Charleston, to begin dealing with postwar South Carolina. One of the first debates they had was to figure out how to deal with those who had been loyal to the British during the war. A compromise was reached between those who wished to punish the Loyalists and those who wanted to pardon them.

The assembly voted to confiscate the property of several hundred Loyalists who had been most active in fighting against the Patriots. The remainder of the Loyalists were given pardons and allowed to keep their property. The assembly went as far as recommending that the governor offer as much as £300 as a reward, dead or alive, for William Cunningham, who had been a Loyalist leader. They also suggested £100 rewards for a number of other Loyalists.

When 12 Loyalists were given 20 days to give up their plantations and then ignored the time limit, eight of them were killed by vigilantes. One of Cunningham's lieutenants was tried by Judge Aedanus Burke at Ninety Six. In accordance with the laws passed by the assembly, the judge freed the man. A group of Patriots who

Many slaves in South Carolina escaped during the Revolutionary War. Some slaves lived in quarters similar to this restored two-room building, one of two on the Hopsewee Plantation in Georgetown County, South Carolina. *(Library of Congress, Prints and Photographs Division [HABS, SC,22-GEOTO.V, 3A-1])*

John Mathews
(1744–1802)

John Mathews was typical of many Patriots of his day. He served as a lieutenant in the South Carolina provincial regiment and fought against the Cherokee. During the Revolution, he became a captain in the Colleton County Regiment of the South Carolina Militia. His first political position was in the provincial congress that met to discuss participation in the First Continental Congress and ways to obtain self-government for the people of South Carolina. From 1778 through 1781, he was a member of the Second Continental Congress.

When he became governor in 1782, he saw to it that the militiamen were kept out of Charleston during the British evacuation. This was done because many were concerned that the militia would seek reprisals against the departing British soldiers and their Loyalist supporters. As governor, he signed a law that gave the state the right to seize the property of a number of Loyalists who had been extremely active in fighting the Patriots. Later, the Treaty of Paris between the United States and Great Britain would call for amnesty for all Loyalists.

claimed that the man had murdered their relatives after the battle at Hay's Station waited for the judge to leave and then hung the Loyalist.

In the Low Country, people were more willing to forgive the Loyalists, who were often forced to assist the British. Up Country, the Loyalist forces had been used against the people living there, and there was a much stronger desire for revenge. Along the frontier, they also had to contend with numerous bandits who took advantage of the lack of an organized military or law enforcement to prey on the small isolated farms.

In 1781 and 1782, the Cherokee, who had been forced to give up a large part of their territory in 1778, tried to get it back. They attacked along the frontier near Ninety Six and in Georgia. General Pickens, who had led the guerrilla fighting in the western part of the state, gathered a force of almost 400 cavalry from South Carolina and Georgia and took the fight into the remaining Cherokee lands. After burning villages and killing numerous Cherokee, the Cherokee were once again defeated. They continued to lose land as settlers from other colonies flooded into the frontier to start new farms.

Known for his participation in a guerrilla campaign to help colonial forces regain control of South Carolina, General Andrew Pickens fought and defeated the Cherokee when they tried to reclaim land they had been forced to surrender in 1778. *(Library of Congress, Prints and Photographs Division [LC-USZ61-70])*

DEBTS AND DEBTORS

During the war, especially after the capture of Charleston by the British in 1780, the economy of South Carolina was completely disrupted. In addition, the state borrowed heavily to finance the war. At the end of the war, the state of South Carolina was more than $5.3 million in debt. This amounted to the highest debt per capita of any of the 13 states. Only Massachusetts and Virginia came close to having as much debt. However, both colonies had many more people than South Carolina.

Low Country planters were in favor of a strong central government because they believed it would be able to repay the state's war debt. Many of those same planters were the ones the state had borrowed from during the war. Up Country, people were more suspicious of a strong central government. When it was time to debate a new constitution, those who were pro and con would divide between those in the backcountry and in the Low Country.

The planters of South Carolina were faced with another problem after the war. They needed to borrow money to rebuild their plantations and replant their fields. The only people who had money and were willing to give them credit were the same merchants they had been dealing with before the war. Partial crop failures in 1783 and 1784 made the situation for the planters even more difficult. Before the war, South Carolina had shipped around 129,000 barrels of rice a year. In 1783 and 1784, they shipped only 50,000 barrels of rice.

In addition to the bad rice harvest, the British had found a cheaper source of indigo in colonial India. This meant that South

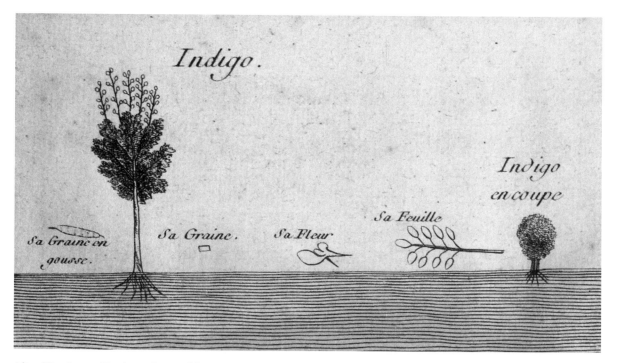

After Eliza Lucas Pinckney learned how to cultivate indigo plants in South Carolina, the crop became a source of wealth for many colonists. *(National Archives of Canada)*

Carolina growers could not make as much money from their indigo crop. The South Carolinians were making progress on governing the state, but they needed a strong central government to protect and regulate trade and deal with the state's debt.

Personal debt was soon as big a problem as public debt. Those who had borrowed heavily to rebuild their farms and plantations were having trouble repaying their loans. After the war, there was a general depression in the economy throughout the new United States. In Massachusetts, in 1786 and 1787, a group of farmers protested against problems caused by mounting debt. This has come to be known as Shays's Rebellion. Although there was no organized rebellion in South Carolina, mobs of debtors forced courts to close down to prevent them from prosecuting debt cases.

To try and help the people of South Carolina, the state government took a number of actions. The most significant was to issue £100,000 in paper money. Many of the states as well as the federal government were forced to issue paper money during and after the war. In most instances, paper money had no real value and was just a promise to pay by the government.

Paper money often varied widely in value and usually depreciated, which meant it became worth less and less. However, the assembly in South Carolina made their paper money more stable by backing it up with land. The state gave out loans of £250 to 400 people in exchange for mortgages on their property. Because the paper money was backed by land, it held its value better than paper money in other states.

LIFE IN SOUTH CAROLINA AFTER THE WAR

In many ways, after the war, life in South Carolina returned to the way it had been before the Revolution. The wealthy planters restored their plantations. Many had to buy more slaves to make up for slaves who had run away during the chaos of the war. In fact, the British encouraged slaves to leave, and many were transported out of the colony.

The rest of the state experienced rapid growth after the Revolution. Colonies to the north had filled up while there was still space in the hills and mountains of South Carolina. The growing population put a lot of pressure on the state government to more

Dated March 4, 1833, this watercolor by Canadian Henry Byam Martin depicts a Charleston slave market. *(National Archives of Canada)*

fairly distribute representation. This was done slowly, but eventually representation became proportional. This caused the balance of power to shift away from the wealthy planters and to the owners of the small farms in the interior. In 1790, after 120 years in Charleston, the capital of South Carolina was moved Up Country to Columbia.

Building a Nation

THE ARTICLES OF CONFEDERATION

In 1777, the Second Continental Congress proposed and passed the Articles of Confederation. This document set up a central government that directed the war effort and held the 13 states together. Although the articles became the rule of government during the war, they were not ratified by all the states until 1781.

There was a controversy over the unsettled lands to the west. Some of the colonial charters had included grants that went from the Atlantic coast all the way to the Pacific Ocean. South Carolina's original charter was like that. The states that had no claims in the west felt that states that did should cede their western lands to the federal government. The fear was that states like Virginia and New York, if allowed to hold onto their western claims, would be much more powerful than states without western lands.

Finally, in 1781, the states with western land claims ceded that land to the federal government, and all 13 states ratified the Articles of Confederation. Under the articles, most of the authority rested with the states. Many at the time were concerned that having a strong federal government would just exchange the British tyrant for an American one.

Under the Articles of Confederation, the federal government was able to function in many ways. However, once the war ended, it became more and more obvious that the government under the articles could not solve a number of the problems faced by the states. Rather than working as one nation, the states often found themselves competing for trade and creating their own systems for charging import and export duties.

The regulation of trade and the ability of the federal government to create taxes were two powers that many in South Carolina wanted the federal government to have. South Carolina's agricultural economy was tied closely to overseas trade. As a single state, South Carolina had little power to negotiate with its trading partners. Also, without the power to create taxes, the federal government would never be able to assume the state's debt from the war. Many wealthy South Carolinians had loaned the state money during the war and would not get paid back without federal help to the state.

Under the articles, the federal government was not allowed to maintain a standing army, which many also saw as a problem. States such as South Carolina that were still having problems with Native Americans along the frontier wanted a federal military to help them as they continued to take land claimed by Native Americans. As talk began about strengthening the Articles of Confederation, many in South Carolina were concerned that a strong central government would try to do away with slavery.

In spite of all these concerns, South Carolina was one of the leaders in pushing for a stronger federal government. Charles Pinckney, who was a delegate to the Continental Congress, established a committee to look at the articles and suggest changes. The committee proposed seven amendments to the Articles of Confederation. Although the Congress did not adopt Pinckney's amendments, they helped point out the shortcomings of the Articles of Confederation.

Charles Pinckney represented South Carolina at the Second Continental Congress. *(Library of Congress, Prints and Photographs Division [LC-USZ61-290])*

Charles Pinckney
(1757–1824)

The Charles Pinckney who was a delegate to the Constitutional Convention was the third distinguished South Carolinian to have that name. Like most of the founding fathers, Pinckney served in the Revolution. He was captured during the siege of Charleston and was in prison until the war ended. His contribution to the creation of the U.S. Constitution has been a mystery for many historians. James Madison of Virginia is usually given much of the credit for the language of the Constitution. Historians have long used Madison's notes as the definitive source for understanding where the ideas behind the Constitution came from. Madison never mentioned Pinckney.

Recent research using the papers of others who were at the Constitutional Convention shows that Pinckney had a much bigger impact than was earlier believed. His plan included many points that were included in the final draft of the Constitution. Some of these include the idea of having a separate House and Senate, counting African Americans as three-fifths of a person, and that impeachment should be done by the House with a subsequent trial in the Senate.

THE ANNAPOLIS CONVENTION

In 1786, a call went out for a convention in Annapolis, Maryland, to consider the problems of regulating trade between the states. All 13 states were invited to send delegates. However, only New York, New Jersey, Delaware, Pennsylvania, and Virginia sent delegations. The representatives from the five states knew they did not have the authority to make decisions for the whole country. They did realize though that the lack of authority of the federal government to regulate trade was creating a number of problems.

Rather than try and change anything, the Annapolis Convention called for a convention to take place in 1787 in Philadelphia to revise the Articles of Confederation. The Annapolis Convention really did not have the authority to call for a constitutional convention, but the Continental Congress thought it was time to revise the articles and supported the recommendation. Delegates from every state except Rhode Island gathered in Philadelphia in May 1787.

Having governed South Carolina during the Revolutionary War and represented the state at the Second Continental Congress, John Rutledge served as a justice on the Supreme Court until his resignation in 1791. *(Library of Congress, Prints and Photographs Division [LC-USZ62-91143])*

THE CONSTITUTIONAL CONVENTION

By the time of the Constitutional Convention in 1787, the majority of voters in South Carolina lived in the backcountry. However, representation in the state assembly was still weighted in favor of the Low Country. This is reflected in the fact that South Carolina sent five delegates to the Constitutional Convention, and they were all lawyers and planters from the Low Country. They were Charles Pinckney and his cousins Charles Cotesworth Pinckney and former governor John Rutledge, as well as Pierce Butler and Henry Laurens. By the time of the Constitutional Convention, Henry Laurens had begun to withdraw from public life and chose not to go to the Convention. The South Carolina delegation was very active in the process of creating the new Constitution.

John Rutledge was on five different committees at the Constitutional Convention. He contributed greatly to the final draft of the Constitution. Charles Cotesworth Pinckney worked to come up with a compromise that would benefit the interests of South Carolina on the issues of navigation acts and the slave trade. It was Pierce Butler who suggested that the Constitution should go into effect when nine states ratified it.

Although these contributions were important, it was Charles Pinckney who may have had the greatest influence of all the South Carolina delegates on the Constitution. During the Constitutional Convention, Pinckney made more than 100 speeches on just about every topic. On May 29, 1787, he introduced the Pinckney Plan or Draught that had 31 of the provisions later adopted in the Constitution. He is directly credited with the language in Article 6 of the Constitution that reads, "no religious test shall ever be required as

Henry Laurens
(1724–1792)

Henry Laurens was one of many South Carolinians whose family had been French Huguenots. As a merchant in Charleston, he was extremely successful and highly respected for his honesty and fair dealings. He served in the colonial legislature before the Revolution and was active in the political struggles for independence. During the war years, he served twice as the president of the Continental Congress.

In 1780, the Congress sent him as its representative to the Netherlands to get additional financing for the war with Britain. While en route, his ship was captured by the British navy, and he was taken to London as a prisoner. He spent 15 months locked in the Tower of London, where he was poorly treated and became quite ill. When he was put on trial, he was unable to stand on his own. Despite his weakened condition, he is reported to have told the court that he was "a citizen of the united, free, and independent states of North America, and will not do any act which shall involve me in an acknowledgement of subjection to this realm."

He was freed in 1781, having been exchanged for Charles, Lord Cornwallis, who had surrendered at Yorktown on October 19, 1781, after the last battle of the War for Independence. Laurens's health never fully recovered after his stay in the Tower of London.

a Qualification to any Office or public Trust under the authority of the United States."

One of the biggest controversies at the Constitutional Convention was how the states would be represented in the federal congress. Under the Articles of Confederation, each state got one vote. At the Constitutional Convention, the delegates broke into two main sides. Virginia, the largest state, put forth a plan that called for states to be represented based on population. The delegates from New Jersey, which was one of the smallest states, presented their own plan that called for states to be represented equally.

The South Carolina delegation favored the Virginia Plan. South Carolina was growing rapidly and felt it would benefit most from proportional representation. Rutledge led the delegation on this point and also called for slaves to be counted for representational purposes. The population of the Low Country in South Carolina was still over 70 percent African-American slaves.

It looked like the Convention had reached an impasse. Then the Connecticut delegation came up with a compromise that is known as the Connecticut plan or the Great Compromise. Under this plan, the federal legislature would have two parts. The first would be the Senate, and it would have two senators from each state. The compromise also called for a House of Representatives that would give states a varying number of representatives based on population. This is the way Congress continues to function today.

African-American slaves outnumbered white colonists in South Carolina until the end of the 18th century. The buildings shown here are typical slave quarters located in the vicinity of Charleston. *(Library of Congress, Prints and Photographs Division [HABS, SC, 10-CHAR.V, 10A-1])*

Once they resolved the issue of representation, the Constitutional Convention still had to deal with whether slaves should be counted. After the Revolution, many in the North, where slavery was not an important part of the economy, wanted to do away with slavery. In the South, slaves were still seen as a necessary source of labor for the plantations. Many northerners expressed concern that states such as South Carolina and Georgia could increase their representation in the House by buying more slaves.

Charles Cotesworth Pinckney argued that part of the federal government's job was to protect property and that it should therefore recognize slaves as part of the population. Finally, the Convention reached a compromise. Slaves would be counted, but each slave would only count as three-fifths of a person. The compromise also called for the population to be recounted every 10 years and the number of seats in the House reapportioned based on the federal census. The first U.S. census was held in 1790 and has been held every 10 years since.

The South Carolina delegation was in the middle of one final controversy before the Constitution was sent to the states. Ten of the 12 states at the Convention were willing to abolish the slave trade. Only South Carolina and Georgia were adamant that the slave trade was critical to their states. At first, South Carolina refused to consider compromise. There was one remaining concession that South Carolina wanted. They wanted the state to be free from export taxes. Their economy was dependent on the export of the crops raised on their plantations. When the convention agreed to have the federal government regulate interstate

Preamble to the U.S. Constitution

We the People of the United States, in Order to form a more perfect Union, establish Justice, insure domestic Tranquility, provide for the common defence, promote the general Welfare, and secure the Blessings of Liberty to ourselves and our Posterity, do ordain and establish this Constitution for the United States of America.

trade, South Carolina gave in, and the delegation agreed to allow the slave trade to end in 20 years.

On September 17, 1787, the new Constitution was accepted by the Convention, and it was signed by all but three of those still present. All four South Carolina delegates—Charles Pinckney, Charles Cotesworth Pinckney, John Rutledge, and Pierce Butler—signed the Constitution. It was now up to the states to ratify it.

SOUTH CAROLINA
The Eighth State

In May 1778, South Carolina held a convention to ratify the U.S. Constitution. When they met, seven states had already ratified and only two more were needed to make the new Constitution law. Like the state assembly, the ratification convention was dominated by representatives from the Low Country. Many have speculated that had the Up Country farmers been in the majority at the ratifying convention, South Carolina would have had a very difficult time ratifying the Constitution.

The small farm owners in the backcountry were not concerned with issues of trade and payment of state debts. They mostly wanted to be left to live and work on their own. The conflict between the Low Country and the Up Country continued to dominate South Carolina politics. However, on May 23, 1788, the delegates to the convention in Charleston voted 149 to 73 in favor of the Constitution. South Carolina became the eighth state to ratify, and a month later the new Constitution went into effect when New Hampshire became the ninth state to ratify.

South Carolina Time Line

ca. 13,000 B.C.

★ The first Native Americans arrive in South Carolina.

1521

★ Lucas Vázquez de Ayllón, the Spanish explorer, reaches the present-day South Carolina, probably on Winyah Bay near present-day Georgetown. The attempt at establishing a colony fails.

1540

★ The Spanish explorer Hernando de Soto passes through present-day South Carolina with a force of 600 and claims it as part of Florida.

1562

★ Jean Ribault leads French Huguenots and establishes Charlesfort on Port Royal Sound, near the present-day Parris Island at Beaufort.

1563

★ The French settlement is abandoned by starving colonists.

1566

★ The Spanish establish Fort San Felipe, or Santa Elena, on what is now Parris Island. It becomes a Spanish trading center.

1587

★ The Spanish withdraw from San Felipe.

early 1600s

★ There are roughly 46 separate tribes in the region, with the Cherokee and the Catawba the largest groups.

1663

★ A charter is granted by King Charles II to the "True and Absolute Lords Proprietors of Carolina," including Sir John Colleton, Sir William Berkeley, Sir Anthony Ashley Cooper (these three were most instrumental in getting the grant), also Edward Hyde, the earl of Clarendon; George, duke of Albemarle; John, Lord Berkeley, brother of William; Sir George Carteret; and William, Lord Craven.

1669

★ **July 21:** The Lords Proprietors of Carolina issue the Fundamental Constitutions, with 128 articles for governing South Carolina, recommending South Carolina have an executive council made up of noblemen and proprietors and an assembly elected from colonists who owned more than 500 acres.

★ **October:** Three ships with 92 settlers head for Carolina from England; two ships are lost in storms.

1670

★ **March:** The settlers land at present-day Beaufort, where the Proprietors want them to build their settlement. The leader of the Kiawah recommends they move 80 miles north to a spot with a better location with a better harbor, which was also better for farming and farther from the Spanish.

★ **April:** The settlers move north. The first English colony in South Carolina is established at Albemarle Point on the Ashley River, with around 100 English settlers and at least one African slave. Soon the governor brings a family of enslaved Africans, called John Senior, John Junior, and Elizabeth, to the colony. Roughly one in three colonists is African. The colony is named Carolina for King Charles II.

1670–1750

★ The Native American populations sharply decline; some die of European diseases while others move west.

1672

★ **spring:** The ship *William and Ralph* arrives with the first shipment of a bushel of rice. Rice is South Carolina's first plantation crop.

1679

★ **December:** The Lords Proprietors order a move to Charles Towne at the confluence of the Ashley and Cooper Rivers.

1680

★ Better quality rice seed reaches South Carolina, which enables large-scale rice cultivation.

1700

★ **November 16:** The first public library in America opens in Charles Towne.

1708

★ **September 17:** The governor issues a census that shows blacks are in the majority.

1710

★ Carolina is divided into North Carolina and South Carolina.

1715

★ **April:** The Yamasee War begins. Yamasee kill settlers near Port Royal.

1719

★ **December 10:** The South Carolina Assembly becomes the "Assembly of the People," a first step toward a proprietary revolution.

by 1720

★ The African slave population is double that of the free white population.

1721

★ **May:** The first royal governor, Francis Nicholson, arrives. The proprietors wait until September 29, 1729, to surrender the title.

1730

★ The royal governor, Robert Johnson, develops the Township Plan to encourage settlement "Up Country," which promises 50 acres for each person, waives taxes (quitrents) for 10 years, and gives a food and equipment bounty for two years.

1730s and 1740s

★ The Up Country is settled, with roughly 2,500 people, mainly from what would become Germany as well as Switzerland, and

Britain. Two of the nine towns, Orangeburg and Williamsburg, are the most successful.

1730–39

★ There are roughly 20,000 enslaved Africans brought to South Carolina.

1739

★ **September 9:** The Stono Rebellion, the first violent slave uprising, with about 100 Africans under "Jemmy," take firearms 20 miles south of Charles Towne. They try to gain momentum but are defeated by whites led by the lieutenant governor. The revolt is put down, and 60 African-American slaves are executed.

1740

★ **May 10:** The Black Codes of 1740 are issued. The codes outline the race situation until the Civil War. It forbids blacks to travel without written permission; grow their own food; hold meetings without whites; learn to read; use drums, horns, or other loud instruments with which they might communicate.

1760

★ **February 1:** Cherokee kill settlers at Long Canes, near Ninety Six.

1762

★ **September 13:** Governor Boone refuses to seat Christopher Gadsden in the assembly, which triggers conflict between the governor and the assembly.

1765

★ The Stamp Act is protested by Charleston's Sons of Liberty.

1767

★ **May:** James Hawker of HMS *Sardoine* capture the Sloop *Active,* which causes conflicts between South Carolina shippers and the authorities, causing most merchants to resist the English.

★ **summer:** The Regulator movement begins in the backcountry.

1768

★ **November 19:** The Massachusetts Circular Letter is voted on by 26 members of the assembly. It is the start of its conflict with English rule.

1774

★ **September 5–October 26:** The First Continental Congress is held in Philadelphia. South Carolina's delegates are Christopher Gadsden, John and Edward Rutledge, Thomas Lynch, and Henry Middleton.

★ **November 1:** South Carolina's "tea party" occurs: A shipload of tea is dumped into Charleston harbor.

1775

★ **January:** A new government is formed with a provincial congress.

★ **September 15:** The assembly is dissolved by Governor Campbell, who flees to a ship in Charleston harbor, bringing about the end of royal government in South Carolina.

★ **November 19–21:** Six hundred patriots fight 1,800 Loyalists in Ninety Six, a town in western South Carolina.

1776

★ **March 26:** South Carolina becomes a state when they adopt a constitution and elect John Rutledge the first governor.

★ **June 28:** The Battle of Fort Moultrie is won by the Americans. This battle led to the palmetto tree's adoption as South Carolina's symbol because the fort was made of palmetto, which was impervious to British cannonballs.

1780

★ **March 29:** Sir Henry Clinton begins a successful two-month siege of Charleston.

★ **May 12:** Charleston falls to the British; the city is pillaged by Hessians and the British.

★ **August 16:** General Gates is defeated at Camden.

★ **October 7:** The Battle of Kings Mountain is fought. American colonel William Campbell defeats the British major Patrick Ferguson.

1780–81

★ "Guerilla warfare" is waged throughout South Carolina by Francis Marion, "the Swamp Fox," in the Low Country; Thomas Sumter, "the Gamecock," in central South Carolina, and Andrew Pickens in western South Carolina.

1781

★ **January 17:** The Battle of Cowpens is fought. Daniel Morgan defeats the British lieutenant colonel Banastre Tarleton.

1782

★ **December 13:** The British evacuate Charleston.

1783

★ The British sign the peace treaty.

★ **November 25:** The British troops withdraw.

1785

★ A committee is established by the General Assembly to consider relocating the state capital to a more central location.

1787

★ **May 23:** The U.S. Constitution, signed by John Rutledge, Charles Cotesworth Pinckney, Charles Pinckney, and Pierce Butler of South Carolina, is ratified by South Carolina.

★ **June 3:** The third state constitution is ratified. It is the first to be ratified by a convention.

★ The capital of South Carolina is moved from Charleston to Columbia, in the center of the state.

South Carolina Historical Sites

BEAUFORT

Fort Frederick   The ruins of this fort built by the British in 1732 were abandoned in 1758.

Address: SC Highway 280, Beaufort, SC 29902

BLACKSBURG

Kings Mountain National Military Park   Thought by historians to be an important turning point in the Revolution in the South, the Patriots were victorious over the British at Kings Mountain. The site includes exhibits, a 27-minute film, and a self-guided battlefield tour.

Address: 2625 Park Road, Blacksburg, SC 29702
Phone: 864-936-7921
Web Site: www.nps.gov/kimo

CAMDEN

Historic Camden Revolutionary War Sites   Camden was occupied by 2,500 British soldiers under Cornwallis for 11 months. The site includes restored buildings and the British military fortifications.

Address: 222 Broad Street, Camden, SC 29020
Phone: 803-432-9841
Web Site: www.historic-camden.org

CHARLESTON

Drayton Hall   Drayton Hall was built between 1738 and 1742. It is the oldest preserved plantation house in America that is open to the public.

Address: 3380 Ashley River Road, Charleston, SC 29414
Phone: 843-769-2600
Web Site: www.draytonhall.org

Heyward-Washington House   A National Historic Landmark, the Heyward-Washington House was built in 1772. It was owned by Thomas Heyward, Jr., who was a signer of the Declaration of Independence. It was rented for George Washington in 1791.

Address: 87 Church Street, Charleston, SC 29403
Phone: 843-722-0354
Web Site: www.charlestonmuseum.com

Magnolia Plantation and Garden   This plantation has been owned by the same family since 1761, when Thomas Drayton arrived from Barbados. It includes the country's oldest garden, established around 1680, and a house built in the 1870s. A 45-minute boat tour of early rice fields is available.

Address: 3550 Ashley Road, Charleston, SC 29414
Phone: 843-571-1266
Web Site: www.magnoliaplantation.com

Middleton Place   This 18th-century plantation includes a museum, gardens, and stable yards.

Address: 4300 Ashley River Road, Charleston, SC 29414
Phone: 843-556-6020
Web Site: www.middletonplace.org

Old Exchange & Provost Dungeon   Delegates to the First Continental Congress were elected at the Old Exchange, which was built between 1767 and 1771. The dungeon was used as a prison during the American Revolution.

> *Address:* 122 East Bay Street at Broad Street, Charleston, SC 29401
> *Phone:* 843-727-2165
> *Web Site:* www.oldexchange.com

Old Powder Magazine   The Old Powder Magazine is the only public building in Charleston from the time of the Lords Proprietors. It was built in 1713 and was used to store munitions until 1748, when it was replaced. It has been restored and has exhibits on early Charleston.

> *Address:* 79 Cumberland Street, Charleston, SC 29401
> *Phone:* 843-722-3767

Thomas Elfe House   Built in the 18th century by Thomas Elfe, an accomplished cabinetmaker.

> *Address:* 54 Queen Street, Charleston, SC 29401
> *Phone:* 843-722-9161

CLEMSON

Hanover House   Hanover House was built in 1716 by a Huguenot family. It was moved to Clemson University from what is now the Santee Cooper dam project when the area was due to be flooded.

> *Address:* PO Box 345605, Clemson, SC 29634
> *Phone:* 864-656-2241
> *Web Site:* www.clemson.edu/welcome/history/hanover.htm

GEORGETOWN

Hopsewee Plantation   Thomas Lynch, Jr., a signer of the Declaration of Independence, was born here. It was built in 1740 and is now open to the public.

Address: 494 Hopsewee Road, Georgetown, SC 29440
Phone: 843-546-7891
Web Site: www.hopsewee.com

HEATH SPRINGS

Hanging Rock   The British, with Loyalists under Major John Carden, were defeated by Patriot militia under General Thomas Sumter at this boulder called Hanging Rock.

Address: S-29-467, Heath Springs, SC 29058

KINGSTREE

Thorntree House   It was built in 1749 by James Witherspoon. In August 1780, it was used as quarters for 100 British dragoons and Loyalists.

Address: Nelson Boulevard, Kingstree, SC 29556
Phone: 843-355-6431

MCCONNELLS

Historic Brattonsville: It is one of the largest living history and restoration sites in South Carolina, with 29 historic buildings, including a working farm. It is also a battle site.

Address: 1444 Brattonsville Road, McConnells, SC 29726
Phone: 803-684-2327
Web Site: www.yorkcounty.org

NINETY SIX

Ninety Six National Historic Site   This site operated by the National Park Service includes the historic Star Fort, the battleground, and a visitor center.

Address: 1103 Highway 248, Ninety Six, SC 29666
Phone: 864-543-4068
Web Site: www.nps.gov/nisi

PENDLETON

Pendleton District Historical, Recreational, and Tourism Commission   Brochures and cassettes are available for walking tours, including the African-American Walking Tour with 10 sites.

Address: 125 E. Queen Street, Pendleton, SC 29670
Phone: 864-646-3782
Web Site: www.pendleton-district.org

ROEBUCK

Walnut Grove Plantation   Built in 1765 by Charles and Mary Moore on land granted them by King George III. During the Battle of Cowpens, their daughter, Kate Moore Barry, worked as a scout for General Daniel Morgan.

Address: 1200 Otis Shoals Road, Roebuck, SC 29376
Phone: 864-576-6546
Web Site: www.spartanarts.org/history

SUMMERTON

Fort Watson   Fort Watson was built by the British on a 35-foot-high Indian mound on the Santee River. The British surrendered to Francis Marion and Henry Lee on April 23, 1781.

Address: US 301 and 15, Summerton, SC 29148

Further Reading

BOOKS

Britton, Tamara L. *The South Carolina Colony*. Edina, Minn.: ABDO, 2001.

Fradin, Dennis Brindell. *The South Carolina Colony*. Chicago: Childrens Press, 1992.

Girod, Christina M. *South Carolina*. San Diego, Calif.: Lucent, 2002.

Hoffman, Nancy. *South Carolina*. Tarrytown, N.Y.: Benchmark Books, 2001.

Weatherly, Myra. *South Carolina*. New York: Childrens Press, 2002.

Weir, Robert M. *Colonial South Carolina*. Millwood, N.Y.: KTO Press, 1983.

WEB SITES

American Local History Network. "South Carolina History." Available online. URL: www.geocities.com/Heartland/Lake.1968/sc-links.html. Downloaded on September 27, 2003.

ICW-NET. "Charleston Area Timeline." Available online. URL: www.charleston-sc.com/history. Downloaded on September 27, 2003.

SCIway. "South Carolina—History and Genealogy Resources." South Carolina's Front Door. Available online. URL: www.

sciway.net/hist/index.html. Downloaded on September 27, 2003.

Software Solutions. "State History." Available online. URL: www3. thingstodo.com/states/SC/history.htm. Downloaded on September 27, 2003.

South Carolina. Department of Parks, Recreation & Tourism. "SC Facts." Available online. URL: www.discoversouthcarolina. com/ scfacts.index.asp. Downloaded on September 27, 2003.

South Carolina State Library. "A Brief History of South Carolina." Available online. URL: www.state.sc.us/scsl/brfhist.html. Downloaded on September 27, 2003.

Index

Page numbers in *italic* indicate photographs. Page numbers in **boldface** indicate box features. Page numbers followed by m indicate maps. Page numbers followed by c indicate time line entries. Page numbers followed by t indicate tables or graphs.